WESTWARD HA!

OR *Around the World in Eighty Clichés*

by S. J. PERELMAN

DRAWINGS BY HIRSCHFELD

 BURFORD BOOKS

Printed in the United States of America

10 9 8 7 6 5 4 3 2 1

Library of Congress Cataloging-in-Publication Data

Perelman, S. J. (Sidney Joseph), 1904–
    Westward ha!, or, Around the world in eighty clichés /
  by S. J. Perelman ; drawings by Hirschfeld.
        p.   cm.
    ISBN 1-58080-067-X (pbk.)
    1. Travel—Humor.   I. Title.
PS3531.E6544W4   1998
813'.52—dc21   98-19493
                                               CIP

*To Frances Goodrich
and Albert Hackett*

Thanks are due to *Holiday* for
permission to reprint material
which has appeared in its pages.

Table of Contents

Ogden Nash, . . . Vernon Duke, . . . and Hirschfeld and I . . . had been sequestered in a room in the Warwick Hotel administering extreme unction to the show

1

Goodbye Broadway, Hello Mal-de-Mer

THE WHOLE sordid business began on a bleak November afternoon a couple of years ago in Philadelphia, a metropolis sometimes known as the City of Brotherly Love but more accurately as the City of Bleak November Afternoons. Actually, the whole business began sixteen years ago, as do so many complex ventures, with an unfavorable astrological conjunction, Virgo being in the house of Alcohol. Late one August day in 1932, I was seated at the Closerie des Lilas in Paris with my wife, a broth of a girl with a skin like damask and a waist you could span with an embroidery hoop. I had had three mild transfusions of a life-giving fluid called Chambéry Fraise and felt a reasonable degree of self-satisfaction. Halfway through my imitation of Rudolph Valentino in *Blood and Sand*, my wife wiped the tears of laughter from her eyes and arose.

"Look, Julian Eltinge," she smiled, naming an actor who had achieved some transitory fame for his powers of mimicry, "*descendez de cette table, salop, et dinons* (come down off that there table, sweetheart, and let us feed the inner man)."

Ever the thrall of a pair of saucy blue eyes, I good-naturedly complied and sprang down with a graceful bound, sustaining a trifling fracture of the spleen. There then ensued a long, absurd debate as to which of us would pay the tab. An innate sense of gallantry prevented me from taking money from a woman, but I stifled it and soon we were bowling along the Boulevard St. Michel in a fiacre. In less time than it takes to build a fourteen-room house, we had crossed the Seine, got lost in Passy, and arrived at a quaint Javanese restaurant in the Rue Pigalle. Lighting my cigarette with a hundred-franc note to show the maître d'hôtel I was a real Parisian boulevardier, I chose an inconspicuous table and ordered *rijstaffel* and a thimbleful of Holland gin for myself and a glass of water for my lady. Presently a young woman I knew, who reported the *haute couture* for several American magazines, approached, followed by a gentleman. My years in the Ochrana had so trained me to absorb vital details that I saw at once he had a beard.

"This is Hirschfeld," said the fashion writer, "the theatrical caricaturist of the *New York Times*." I instantly scented a touch and, furtively secreting my wallet in my wife's stocking, pretended to be stone deaf. The young woman's tongue, ordinarily a quiet, reserved sort of chap, was wagging more than its usual wont.

"Hirschfeld wants to do a caricature of you," she said brightly.

"*Je comprends pas*," I shrugged, "me stony, you savvy? Plenty bankruptcy along me."

"It's free," explained Hirschfeld, who up to that time had been mute. My deafness vanished forthwith, and turning my good profile to him, I waited patiently whilst his pencil flew. In no time at all—five minutes, to be exact—we were laughing and chatting away as though we had known each other five minutes.

Hirschfeld left for the States that night, just before the check arrived, and I did not see him for a spell. One day in New York, I ran into him outside a little specialty shop in the Forties where I had just bought a black girdle with rose panels and a bias-cup brassière for my mother. We had a stoup of kumiss together and renewed our friendship. Whether he stole the cuff-links I missed subsequently, I would prefer not to say, but it seemed more than coincidence. Nevertheless, I am one who forgives easily, and it was hardly more than eleven years before I found myself one morning excitedly telephoning him.

"I've got an idea for a musical comedy, old man," I said directly (I rarely beat about the bush). "Meet me at the Lafayette Coffee Rooms at one o'clock." Had Hirschfeld not met me at the Lafayette Coffee Rooms at one o'clock, this might never have been written. Another thing that might never have been written, if it gives twenty-three despondent investors any comfort, was a musical comedy named *Sweet Bye and Bye*, which closed in Philadelphia like a ten-cent mousetrap the day this story opens.

Ogden Nash, who wrote the lyrics of *Sweet Bye and Bye*, Vernon Duke, the tunesmith responsible for its airs, and Hirschfeld and I, who spawned the libretto, had been sequestered in a room in the Warwick Hotel there for nineteen hours administering extreme unction to the show. At length our efforts were unavailing; as the turkey lay cold and lifeless on the operating table before us, Nash retired to his room to hang himself with a dangling participle. Duke returned to writing singing commercials, and we groped our way to the Anguish Room of the Warwick for a final cup of coffee. We were both sobbing brokenly into a wisp of cambric when the editor of a journal named *Holiday*, a furtive personality in a hand-me-down suit and linen of dubious cleanliness, shambled up to us. In an effort to shatter his torpor, I informed him that the show had just breathed its last. Our plight would have moved a heart of stone, and he certainly had it.

"What are you going to do now?" he inquired, stroking Hirschfeld's beard thoughtfully.

"Oh, I don't know," I replied carelessly, "I may join the Foreign Legion, or, on the other hand, I may take a hot bath." My companions looked around startled, under the impression that Noel Coward had spoken, but of course Coward was nowhere to be seen, as it was I who had spoken. Suddenly I became conscious of the editor's close scrutiny.

"Why don't you take a trip around the world for us?" he proposed. There was a moment of portentous silence. When a man you scarcely know suggests a trip lasting nine months and covering twenty-seven countries, you are justified in leaping to one of four assumptions: first, that he is an impostor; second, that he is hopelessly in love with your wife and will go to any lengths to get you out of the country; third, that you have blundered by mistake into an Alfred Hitchcock film; and fourth, that you have succumbed to a combination of *ennui de moyen âge*, wanderlust, paranoia, and brandy. Almost immediately, however—in fact, just as soon as the waiters had finished applying cold towels to my forehead—I regained my aplomb.

"All right, if you insist," I consented, stifling a yawn, "I suppose it's weak of me, but I just can't refuse you anything. Silly, isn't it?"

And before you could say "bo" to a goose, the whole matter had been arranged. Hirschfeld, who had done the Giant Swing once before, was unquestionably the ideal person to share my stateroom and illustrate our experiences; besides, I needed someone to protect me from whatever sultry womanhood, bloodthirsty brigands, and carnivorous fauna lay in wait. His qualifications were obvious: a pair of liquid brown eyes, delicately rimmed in red, of an innocence to charm the heart of the fiercest aborigine, and a beard which would engulf anything from a tsetse fly to a Sumatra tiger. In short, a remarkable combination of Walt Whitman, Lawrence of Arabia, and Moe, my favorite waiter at Lindy's.

Our itinerary was soon settled; commandeering an air-mail envelope from the desk clerk, we drew a line west from Hollywood, hemstitching all the areas celebrated by Kipling, Conrad, and Maugham. For one delicious moment I toyed with the possibility of a side trip up to Tibet. My pulses throbbed as I envisioned us entering Shangri-La, our ears loud with the buzz of prayer-wheels, fawned on by the Grand Dalai Lama (played by Sam Jaffe). When Hirschfeld pointed out, however, that a couple of middle-aged aesthetes trained on corned-beef and Dr. Brown's Celery Tonic were ill equipped to ascend the slopes of Kanchanjanga, I reluctantly gave way. Finally our route was complete—Samoa, the Fijis, New Zealand, Australia, the Netherlands East Indies, the Federated Malay States, Siam, Indo-China, India, Iraq, Syria, Palestine, Turkey, Egypt, the Anglo-Egyptian Sudan, British East Africa, the Belgian Congo, North Africa, France, Switzerland, England, and Ireland. We would have included South America, Russia, and China, but my fountain pen, which writes even under hysteria, unexpectedly ran dry.

The financial arrangements, of course, were left to subordinates and bookkeepers, outside of a brief, spirited wrestle in which we kicked, bit, and gouged each other until our skins glowed. Eventually, the magazine grudgingly agreed to settle upon us as expense money a sum sufficient to feed a family of starlings through a Labrador winter. In vain I protested that my dependents would be reduced to beggary; the editor's face remained flinty. "About time those *schleppers* went to work," he grunted. "That brother-in-law of yours hasn't pulled his weight in the boat since you sprung him from Dannemora."

My heart was beating an irregular tattoo the following evening as I entered my apartment in New York, primed to make a dramatic announcement of the trip. I pictured the family's stunned surprise, the entreaties of my wife, the children whimpering at my knee and imploring me not to desert them. Poor little chaps, deprived of a father's wise counsel and love through a cruel caprice of Fate! I resolved at all costs not to yield to my emotions. From the living room, as I tiptoed toward it, came childish merriment, voices uplifted in song. Setting my shoulders squarely, I strode in.

"Well, folks," I said casually, "Daddy's off to the Seven Seas." Unfortunately, at this precise moment my foot encountered a roller skate lying athwart the threshold. As my wife and the dwarfs looked up in astonishment, I ricocheted across the room, clawed ineffectually at the *toile de Jouy* drapes, and stemming myself with a Christiania turn, crashed to the floor, taking a cloisonné vase with me. The memsahib sighed heavily.

"It's no use trying to conceal it any longer, children," she told them. "He drinks."

"Does he beat you, too, Mummy?" demanded the boy, a manly little fellow of ten, as he took a step forward and doubled his fists. "Because if he does, I—I'll—" So fierce was his ire I daresay he would have thrashed me soundly had not his mother interfered; but the good woman soon restored harmony, and, applying a raw beefsteak to my eye to reduce the swelling, I poured out a breathless account of my project. The effect was somewhat lessened by the fact that I was alone in the room, the others having gone to the movies in the interval, but upon their return I broke the great news and apathy was the order of the day. Soon the gentle snores of the household were the only sounds to be heard, and rolling myself in my blanket, I lay awake excitedly anticipating the morrow.

How to describe the days that followed? There was Hirschfeld to be put on the train to Hollywood (and Hirschfeld to be taken off again, when it turned out to be the wrong train); there was Hirschfeld's thirteen-months-old baby to be shipped west to be present at our sailing, though the poor thing was so backward it could not even speak English; it was Hirschfeld this and Hirschfeld that until sometimes I thought I must go mad. I lived in a whirlwind of activity, haunting cut-rate luggage shops for bargains in paper satchels, falsifying declarations for my passport, issuing ukases to my tailors for cummerbunds and stengah shifters. Hardly a day passed that I did not issue at least three ukases, and hardly a day that I did not receive three back informing me that my credit was exhausted. Nevertheless, by judicious shopping I managed to gather a splendid kit for my journey—a machete, a sola topee, a poncho, an apparatus for distilling seawater, and deuce knows what-all. The army-and-navy stores I bought them at will be paid just as soon as the lawyers probate the will of my uncle in Australia, a very wealthy man.

Even the veriest tyro knows that the first consideration of the experienced world traveler is a good set of maps. The air was like wine and my step was springy one fall morning as I pushed open the door of the Aardvark map shop in Radio City. A listless citizen in an alpaca jacket ceased scratching his fundament long enough to survey me vacuously. I outlined my simple needs—a detail map of Melanesia, one of India, and still another of Africa. With an air that clearly implied he found the role of salesman demeaning, he nodded toward a rack. I dug out what I needed and reached for my wallet. To my chagrin, I discovered I had only thirty-seven cents in change. Producing a blank check on the Absconders' and Defaulters' National Bank, in which I am an important depositor, I scribbled out a draft for two dollars and fifty-five cents. The salesman picked it up as though it were infected, vanished into the stockroom, and returned with another incompetent.

"This is our manager, Mr. Register," he said.

"Cass Register," his superior added with an important cough, "at your service. Is this your check?"

"No," I replied sweetly, "it's an old sampler woven shortly after the Deerfield Massacre by Charity Sumpstone, my great-grand-mother fifth removed."

"How's that again?" he frowned, a puzzled expression invading his fat face. I instantly regretted the frivolous line I had taken, and, with extreme civility, requested him to okay the check. He asked for some identification; I drew out various letters of accreditation for the trip, a note from Admiral Halsey asking me to have a collar starched for him in Shanghai, and other trivia of the sort.

"Hm-m-m," he murmured skeptically, "got any other identification? Social Security card?" My wattles flushing a dusty pink, I extended my Pennsylvania driving license. He examined it closely under an infra-red ray, shook his head majestically. "No good—this comes from Pennsylvania."

"Look," I said patiently, "the leather in these shoes I'm wearing comes from the Argentine. But *I* come from New York."

"So do a lot of other dead beats, brother," he remarked with an intimate smile. I disemboweled him with a glance.

"You know, of course," I reminded him, "that it happens to be a State and Federal offense to pass a bad check. Do you think I'd put my neck in the noose for a measly two dollars and fifty-five cents?"

"Well, we get some pretty shifty specimens in here," he replied steadily. Ultimately, by leaving behind a platinum watch and a 25 cc. test-tube of arterial fluid, I won my freedom. I spent the balance of the forenoon in a dark booth at Tim Costello's, reducing my blood pressure with Golden Wedding laced with paraldehyde and weaving dirty limericks around the name of a certain map company.

Purely out of deference to my life insurance company, I underwent the customary routine of inoculations for typhoid, paratyphoid, typhus, smallpox, tetanus, yellow fever, plague, and cholera. A physique hardened in every bodega in Manhattan withstood the shock admirably, except that now and again, without any warning, I abruptly ran a fever of 108 and pitched forward in a dead faint. An infinitely more grueling complication, though, came about quite by accident. One evening, at a musical soirée, I found myself vis-à-vis a young person of the most extravagant charms, whose manner left no doubt that she wished to trifle in the conservatory. I allowed

The customary routine of inoculations for typhoid, paratyphoid, typhus, smallpox, tetanus, yellow fever, plague, and cholera

myself to be beguiled out behind a potted palm, but just as I was slipping my arm around her yielding waist she sharply brought me back to earth. It transpired that she was a contact lens technician and that her interest in my eyes was entirely professional. "We're going to throw away those glasses of yours, Charlie," she announced forcefully. "I wouldn't let you go on a trip like that with those crutches. Report to my web tomorrow morning at ten-fifteen." Sheep that I am, I found myself stretched out at the appointed hour on a surgical table in her office. A sinister Torquemada with a Brooklyn accent was bending over me with what he conceived to be a reassuring manner.

"Now hold still a second, sonny," he said silkily, "we'll just make a little mold of your eyeball—hey presto!" A hoarse cry died still-born in my larynx; simultaneously I felt the impact of hot cobbler's sealing wax on my retina. I reared up like Levi Jackson bucking the Harvard backfield, at the same time kicking outward as in the French *savate*. When the technician had finished probing bits of Erlenmeyer flask and optical glass out of my face, the hands of the clock pointed to four and I was compelled to leave, as it was time for my Malay lesson at the Berlitz School. Promising to return the next afternoon for my try-on—a pledge I had no intention of fulfill-ing—I tottered out.

My reasons for taking Malay were fivefold, the other four of which I seem to have forgotten. The chief object was to get rid of eighty dollars which was burning a hole in my pocket, though I pretended to myself that the language would be indispensable from Australia to Singapore. I also wanted to be able to salt my speech with an occasional picturesque phrase like "Boy, tell Missy's amah to take this chit to the Residency chop-chop."

The first fifteen minutes of the session with Dr. van Oost, my Malay teacher, went off swimmingly. I was compelled to bellow slightly to make myself audible, since the doctor wore a formidable hearing aid, but in a few seconds my accent was indistinguishable from that of a native of Batavia (Batavia, New York, that is). Mid-way through a typical colloquialism, "Boy, beli besok ayam di atas papan tulis" (Boy, buy me tomorrow a chicken in the blackboard),

17

I experienced the distinct sensation of being alternately smothered and roasted. The classroom could not have been at fault; it was over five feet square and had a nice large transom to admit the air. Dr. van Oost's voice gradually began to fade in volume and a rivulet of perspiration coursed down my nose; I realized with a sinking sensation that the typhoid inoculation was taking hold by the moment. I half-rose, plucked ineffectually at my collar, and sank limply into the doctor's arms. Aeons later, I came to in the principal's office, revived by a flabby Mitteleuropean who kept blowing cigar smoke into my face and making pointed references to my manhood.

I acquired my contact lenses a day or two later and they worked superbly. To insert them was but the work of a moment; all I had to do was pry open my eyes with a buttonhook, force the lenses in, and gulp as though swallowing a Chincoteague oyster. The resulting vision was practically 20-20. Everything looked milky and I could drill a photo of Nelson Eddy between the eyes at point-blank range. The lenses also materially enhanced my comeliness; in profile I had the melancholy grandeur of a carp at Fontainebleau. The effect on family and friends was equally gratifying. My children turned to stone at the first glimpse of their sire, and then broke wildly for cover. It took a fabulous bribe to tempt them out from underneath the bed. The mem, more articulate, put her opinion in a single succinct sentence.

"Stunning," she observed. "You certainly ought to set Singapore aflame with those immies in your head." Perhaps the most practical suggestion came from an old college classmate I met on the street.

"Why don't you have another one made up?" he proposed.

"Why? They're unbreakable—they're made of plastic."

"Sure," he agreed, "but it's a great chance for a shell game. If you meet an easy mark on your travels, you can always whip 'em out of your eyes, shuffle 'em, and say, 'Now, under which one of these is my cornea?'"

In the cold gray light of a winter dawn they gathered at the airport to bid me Godspeed, the gallant band of relatives who had stuck by me through thick and thin like leeches. Tears streamed down the cheeks of cousins and nephews who now would have to go back to work. One crapulous uncle, last employed shortly before the Battle of Cerro Gordo, was especially eloquent. "Won't seem like the same place any more without you," he snuffled. He was dead right; his days of free-loading were over.

Only my immediate family betrayed its sincere feelings. My wife looked ten years younger already; the sudden release from years of tyranny acted on her like vintage champagne. The children's eyes danced at the prospect of the destruction they could now cause with impunity. They signalized their freedom by firing off cap pistols in my ear, sprinkling sneeze powder over the luggage, and generally behaving with such winsomeness that I promptly made a note to cut them off without a farthing.

The motors roared, a final embrace, and we were aloft. The airstrip receded; I was alone in the empyrean except for two dozen other escapists speeding toward Cathay. Seventy minutes later, my wife heard the shrill repeated ring of the telephone. She laid down her glass, picked up the receiver. The voice of the man she loved drifted faintly over the wire.

"What?" she demanded mystified. "Are you in Bali already?"

"Well—er—not exactly," I hesitated. "The plane was grounded in Camden. I'm calling you from Joe's Coffee Pot."

"That's nice," she replied. "Give my regards to the other loafers." And she hung up. I drew my balmacaan a bit tighter about me, kicked over a spittoon, and went slowly up the tarmac. From now on I would have to play it solo, a high heart set resoluté and unafraid against the unknown.

2

Please Don't Give Me Nothing
to Remember You By

WEIGHTLESS, imponderable, as idle as a painted ship upon a painted ocean, the great airliner hung high in the thin air above the Sierra Nevadas, its wolfish snout strained toward the paling horizon. Two hundred miles away, in the broad plain washed by the Pacific, lay its goal, the Athens of the West, the mighty citadel which had given the world the double feature, the duplexburger, the motel, the hamfurter, and the shirt worn outside the pants—the Great Pueblo, the City of Our Lady the Queen of the Angels—Los Angeles. Thirty-five hundred feet below the plane, two turkey vultures clung to a snowy crag and picked idly at some bones.

"This sure was a delicious scenario writer," ruminated the elder, stifling a belch. "You'd have to go all the way to Beverly Hills for one like him."

"Listen," said his companion, "that bad I don't need *anything*." He turned, peering up at the receding roar of motors. "Well," he observed sourly, "there goes the morning flight to L.A. Same old cargo of hopheads, hustlers, and movie satraps."

"Ah, what the hell," said the first indulgently. "They're just people."

"So was Dillinger people," snapped the other. "So was Charlie Ponzi. I tell you, it's to chill the marrow. I wouldn't eat one of those creeps up there if I was starving. Jeez, I'm not fastidious, but you've got to draw the line *somewhere*."

And yet, shrewd though his estimate of the flagship's passengers was, the bird was not wholly right. For among that raffish, dissolute

crew speeding toward the sea was one who by his very goodness retrieved them all. A simple, unpretentious man of a grave but kindly mien, his gaunt profile blended the best features of Robinson Jeffers, Lou Tellegen, Pericles, and Voltaire. A keen, humorous eye sparkled above a seamed cheek which had been tanned a rich oleomargarine at the Copacabana and the Stork Club. His loosely woven tweeds were worn with all the easy authority of a man accustomed to go into a pawnshop, lay down his watch, and take his four dollars home with him. As he sat there, relaxed and skyborne, it was the type of subject that would have inspired Monet or Whistler to reach for his palette—the humble dignity of the wayfarer, the pearly effulgence of the clouds, the sense of perfect equilibrium between man and nature.

Nonetheless, under my seemingly placid exterior—for let us not dissemble longer, dear reader, it was indeed myself I have taken the liberty to describe—behind my outwardly cool mask, I say, I was prey to a hundred conflicting sensations. Hypertension, nausea, anticipation of the events in store for me, the dull ache of parting with my creditors—a host of emotions strove for mastery within my breast. In less than an hour, I would be in the fabulous film colony of Hollywood, on the first leg of my journey around the world. Soon I would be clasping the flabby hands of erstwhile colleagues in the movie industry, listening to the purr of their ulcers, and noting with satisfaction their paunches and the crow's-feet around their eyes. A wave of nostalgia engulfed me as I remembered the decade I had spent writing motion pictures; a suspicious moisture glittered in my orb. What a splendid, devil-may-care band we had been in the Thirties, brave lads and lasses all—ever ready to cut a competitor's throat or lick a producer's boot, ever eager to conform our opinions to those in authority, ever alert to sell out wife, child, and principle to attain the higher bracket, the fleecier polo coat, the more amorous concubine. Wave a pay-check at us and we could turn in our own wheelbase, strip ourselves inside out like a glove; the most agile, biddable, unblushing set of mercenaries since the Hessians. Five years ago, standing with one foot on the eastbound *Chief*, I had addressed the small party of sycophants come to wish me farewell.

"Wild horses," I had announced with slow emphasis, "wild horses tied tail to tail, mark you, will never drag me back to this leprous, misbegotten kraal. May a trolley-car grow in my stomach if ever again I put foot west of the Great Continental Divide." But here I was, a little older, a little grayer, and a little poorer; and as the first straggling vineyards of San Bernardino appeared in the distance, my impatience grew so acute as to resemble the effects of nembutal.

The plane slid smoothly down the asphalt, wheeled, and shuddered to a stop. Tom Swift (for it was indeed he who had piloted the craft on our perilous transcontinental dash) emerged from the cockpit, pulling off his helmet and goggles. "Well, fellows, we made it," he said quietly. "Thanks, Tom," I said, "Roger and over." I descended and stretched, drinking in great deep draughts of the characteristic Los Angeles morning effluvia. Outside the terminal, I found that influential friends had provided me with a taxi which, for a trifling sawbuck, bore me to the house in suburban Bel-Air I would inhabit during my stay. En route, I chatted with the *izvozchik*, a strange pinhead with a face like a sculpin and a chauffeur's linen duster, who drove at breakneck pace; not once did the needle on the speedometer fall below ten miles an hour. I asked if he had ever driven a car before. He shook his head.

"I'm learning, though," he assured me. "I can go around corners now. Tomorrow I'm going to take a lesson in backing up." There was a short silence while I fingered my beads.

"How long before you get a driver's license?" I asked.

"Oh, I've got plenty of *them*," he said easily. "They give 'em to you here when you buy a car. They do that everywhere."

"Not in New York they don't, Buster," I rejoined.

"New York?" he repeated, puzzled. "Where's that?" I let the conversation languish; I realized with overpowering finality that from here in, I was in *partibus infidelium*. Somehow it recalled the remark once made to me by the wife of a picture producer. A native Angeleno and graduate of the Hollywood High School, she had never been anywhere but Palm Springs, Lake Arrowhead, Tia Juana, and similar local fly-traps. One rainy day, on a bearskin rug before a glowing fire, she confessed her profound discontent, her overwhelm-

Hollywood Native: Female

ing *Weltschmerz*. I suggested that she take a trip around the world.

"Oh, I know," returned the lady, yawning with ennui, "but there's so many other places I want to see first."

Safely installed in my Mediterranean palazzo in Bel-Air, I hastily boarded the windows to exclude the blasted sunshine and telephoned Hirschfeld, my traveling companion, who had reined into town the day before. He had just spent three weeks in San Francisco trying to book passage to Samoa and was inclined to be gloomy.

"It's no dice," he said dejectedly. "The next boat doesn't leave for five months. Even if we could get there, the only transportation between Samoa and the Fijis is outrigger canoe."

"Then let's go to Tahiti," I proposed. "They say that's an island paradise."

"Who says so?" rasped Hirschfeld.

"Er—the washroom attendant at '21,'" I confessed. "But I know it's true. Did you see *The Moon and Sixpence*?"

"No, but I saw Tahiti," he said, "and it's just like Washington Heights. It's full of beat-up ukulele players and cheap grifters; they've got a Whelan drugstore on every block."

"Well," I said, "we've got to get to New Zealand somehow."

"What for?" he demanded. "If you've ever been in Nutley, New Jersey, you know what it's like."

"Now wait," I said impatiently, "I don't know about Tahiti and New Zealand, but you can't shrug off Australia. Kangaroos—boomerangs—superbly formed young women riding surfboards down under—"

"Bah," said Hirschfeld contemptuously. "Another Far Rockaway. Listen, brother, get yourself organized. The place we want to head for is Bali. I lived there eight months and it's heaven." In a few badly-chosen words, he sketched a picture of a veritable Garden of Eden inhabited by innocent, droll folk who asked nothing but the privilege of barbecuing suckling pigs for us, twining hibiscus in our hair, and entertaining us with superb ritual dances. Such was his eloquence that I could almost hear the beat of the surf on the beaches, smell the dizzying scent of nutmeg borne on a zephyr from the Moluccas. By the time we met at the travel agency that afternoon, I was moving with the languorous feline grace of the true Balinese; passers-by in the lobby paused to exchange admiring whispers at my sinuous slant-eyed charm. So complete was the illusion, indeed, that one young woman in the elevator threw discretion to the winds and flirted boldly with me. Naturally, I avoided her eyes, since her escort was staring suspiciously at me, and merely returned a discreet pinch and my telephone number. She must have been an illiterate, however, as I failed to hear from her subsequently. It may be, on the other hand, that her escort poisoned her mind against me in some way that I cannot comprehend. In any case, she was not very good-looking, and I probably escaped a dangerous entanglement by a hair's breadth.

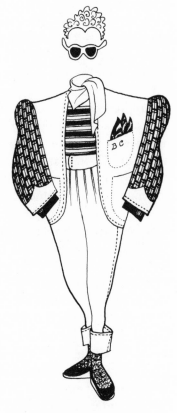

Hollywood Native: Male

It took only nine days of tramping the steamship offices to convince us how romantic we were and how plastic our itinerary would have to be. Not only were the Netherlands East Indies aflame, but thousands of évacués were piled up in San Francisco seeking passage back to their homes. On Fisherman's Wharf alone, we learned, were eight hundred missionaries drinking themselves blind while they awaited transshipment to their posts. What made it a particularly neat mathematical problem was the fact that only seven freighters were scheduled to sail for the East within the next five weeks, each carrying twelve passengers. Eventually, through a display of guile that would have done credit to Talleyrand, we wheedled the last two berths aboard a vessel named the *Marine Flier,* bound for Chinwangtao, Shanghai, Hong Kong, and Singapore. Then, with tickets snugly stowed in our shiny new passport cases and malodorous five-cent cigars sputtering in our faces, we set about preparing in earnest for the grand tour.

Obviously our first and most vital requisite for such widely disparate locales as Cambodia, Northern India, and French Equatorial Africa was a proper medical kit. Hirschfeld, whether through ignorance or bravado, laid in nothing but a package of band-aids and a box of "Cow Brand" bicarbonate of soda. Luckily for him, I had had two years of pre-medical training before switching over to the commercial course, and I was able to give him the benefit of expert scientific knowledge. At an army surplus store on South Broadway, I picked up an excellent second-hand first-aid unit. Some of the bandages had been used and would have to be rinsed out, but the forceps, tourniquet, and iodine applicators were in mint condition. I also purchased a pair of surgical gloves and a can of ether in case my confrere was stricken in the veldt and I had to operate on him by candlelight. Oddly enough, instead of being grateful for my vigilance, Hirschfeld turned sullen. From several rather coarse comments he made, I got the impression he doubted my dexterity. "If I have my choice, pal," he sneered, "I'll take tetanus." I realized, of course, that his attitude was characteristic of the typically superstitious and uninformed layman, and secreted the kit in my baggage against a future emergency.

It then occurred to us that, like sandhogs entering a decompression chamber, we ought to accustom ourselves beforehand to the geographical extremes we would encounter—the steaming jungles of Cochin China, the sun-baked wastes of the Sahara, the crocodile-infested waters of Lake Chad, and the woman-infested cafés of Port Said. What more ideal test laboratory than Hollywood, which in a hundred films had re-created every possible latitude, every conceivable hazard? I forthwith approached a number of prominent Hollywood directors and, posing our problem, begged their assistance. To a man, those of them who could understand English responded to our plea. Theirs were names to conjure with—Leon Gordon, who had made the great sociological South Seas study, *White Cargo*; John Farrow, whose *China* had done so much to widen the gulf between that country and ours; James Whale, director of *Green Hell*, which had won the Spyros Oblivion prize for the most torpid picture of 1938; Zoltan Korda, creator of *Sahara*, one of the most sought-after personalities in Hollywood, to say nothing of the Sahara; and Henry King, director of *Stanley and Livingstone*, which, by an almost unbelievable coincidence, was released the very same day luminal was first synthesized. A few telephone calls, a crisp word or two spoken into a subordinate's ear, and instantly the complex machinery of the studios was in motion.

In the three ensuing days, Hirschfeld and I underwent every possible vicissitude the globe-trotter can experience short of complete annihilation. We were stood up in wind tunnels and subjected to fearful man-made simoons, flung into fetid marshes and pelted with coconuts. We were shipwrecked, marooned, waylaid by banditti, captured by head-hunters, charged by rhinos, and overcharged by hotelkeepers. We were drenched, fried, parboiled, roasted, steamed, and sautéed. In one appalling morning, I was made to ride every form of conveyance from a camel to a Swiss funicular; though I pleaded for mercy, I was even carried piggy-back through some artificial saw-grass by a certified Swahili. We spent a night in a malaria-infested tent on the Metro back lot, shivered through another in a ruined temple at Paramount, slapping away at bats. Errol

27

Flynn taught us how to woo a brown-skinned Burmese lass, Rex Harrison instructed us in Siamese court etiquette, Johnny Weismuller coached us in the technique of swinging from tree to tree. The final test of our hardihood came when we were permitted to witness a combat virtually never seen: a fight between a mongoose and a cobra, with the victor engaging a motion-picture executive, or jackal. As the vanquished mongoose crept away to die, we knew that after this whatever terrors the future held would fade into insignificance.

Our embarkation date was almost upon us when we suddenly realized we had been neglecting the social life of Hollywood. Out came our dinner coats, green with age, their lapels still flecked with soup-stains from some forgotten banquet. We let it be bruited about that we were available for cotillions, drags, routs, buffets, and balls. The news had an electric effect; within three days, our mail was filled with sample swatches of cloth from Beverly Hills tailors, pamphlets offering to charter hundred-foot Diesel twin-screw yachts sleeping twelve, and solicitations from relief committees. Ultimately, several more courageous hostesses decided to risk social obloquy and invited us to dine, and from then on we lived at fever pitch.

The most marked change wrought during my five years' absence from Hollywood was the constant preoccupation, everywhere we went, with art. Dinner conversation, formerly compounded of blistering speculations about the love life of one's friends, now consisted of squabbles over the Post-Impressionists and brisk trading in gouaches. Onetime vaudeville bookers who would have considered Frederic Remington's "The Last Water-hole" a bit highbrow were collecting Picasso and Braque by the carload; a new anecdote about Renoir was esteemed far more than one about Ava Gardner. Every time we entered a home in Beverly Hills, we were met with a stench of turpentine and prussic blue that well-nigh swept us off our pins.

The evening with Midge and Dorian Schlagober was typical from the moment we rang the doorbell. A set of chimes within promptly went into "Frère Jacques"; some salesman for "Frère

Jacques" door-chimes must have covered Beverly Hills on a bicycle, because they seemed to be standard equipment in no less than nine houses we visited. Midge Schlagober, an ash blonde with a plunging neckline, swept toward us across the parquet, enveloping us in her fatal charm.

"Too too divine having you," she fluted. "I can't wait for you to see our new Rasmussen." Presuming that she referred to a new kind of deep-freeze mechanism, we started toward the kitchen, but she shepherded us into the living room. Four or five guests, carefully selected with an eye to the length of their studio contracts, were gathered about a finger-painting which could have been executed by any backward boy of nine. They were exclaiming vigorously over its tonality and impasto.

"Yes, it's so—so uninhibited," Midge beamed. "That's what I like about Rasmussen—his freedom. Don't you, Mr. Hirschfeld?"

"Personally," said Hirschfeld, "I think they ought to take it away from him."

"Take what away?" asked Midge with a pained smile.

"His freedom," said Hirschfeld bluntly. There was a short dynamic silence, shattered at last by the entrance of our host, Dorian, his arms piled high with Toulouse-Lautrecs. He bore them with athletic ease, possibly because only six years ago he had similarly borne shoulders of mutton in a Chicago slaughterhouse. But that was before he had written *Dark Abattoir*, the plagiarism of Upton Sinclair's novel which had landed him a $1500-a-week job in pictures.

"I was cleaning out a drawer and found these little things," he simpered. "They're not Lautrec's best period, but they may amuse you." We examined the drawings, which, incidentally, happened to be the most palpable forgeries, and clucked dutifully. When dinner was announced at last, I fatuously supposed we would have done with aesthetics and descend to a more animal plane. I was mistaken. All the way from the hot baked grapefruit to the chocolate soufflé, the company was treated to an exhaustive account by the Schlagobers of the bargain Utrillos they had gleaned on their last visit to New York. The pressure finally became too much for Hirschfeld.

Hollywood Clambake

"Say, men," he remarked, clearing his throat, "I saw a dame with a honey of a shape on Sunset Boulevard today." Midge rose from her chair as if someone had given her a hotfoot.

"Dorian, darling, why don't you show everybody *your* paintings?" she cooed.

"What, does *he* paint too?" I inquired, concealing my agitation.

"Of course," she said haughtily. "All the dealers say he's the most significant primitive since the Douanier Rousseau." As the guests trooped toward Dorian's study uttering broken little cries of expectation, Hirschfeld and I ducked into the powder room and effected an egress, like Tom Sawyer, down a rainspout. Forty minutes later, we were seated in the most ribald burlesque theater in Los Angeles, digging each other in the ribs and roaring with laughter at the *double-entendres* of the comics. He didn't look in the least like one of Rouault's clowns, but that night I could have sworn he was a greater artist than W. C. Fields.

A fine mist hovered over the City of the Walking Dead as we swung up over the Cahuenga Pass and pointed our radiator emblem toward San Francisco. Hirschfeld leaned out and stared pensively at the myriad twinkling lights of Los Angeles.

"You know," he said at length, "somebody once called this town Bridgeport with palms. But I'll tell you something about it just the same."

"What's that?" I asked, never taking my foot off the throttle.

"I'd rather be embalmed here than any place I know," he said slowly. He turned up the collar of his trench coat and lit a cigarette, and in the flare of the match I saw that his tiny pig eyes were bright with tears.

3

Boy Meets Gull

A
T ELEVEN O'CLOCK of a foggy February morning in the year 17——, waterfront loungers in the quaint old seaport town of Bristol, England, might have observed a candid, freckle-faced lad of thirteen, accompanied by a freckle-faced pirate with a freckle-faced parrot on his shoulder, boarding the brig *Hispaniola,* the beginning of a journey which would take its place one day among the major classics of all time. History, once called "that inconstant jade" by Carlyle (not Thomas Carlyle—Gus Carlyle, who used to run the poolroom in Perkasie, Pennsylvania), has a way of repeating herself. Exactly two hundred years later and five thousand miles across the world, waterfront loungers on San Francisco's Embarcadero might have observed a candid lad of forty-three named Perelman, with a portable typewriter and an elastic conscience, accompanied by a bearded pirate named Hirschfeld with a freckled portfolio on his shoulder, boarding the freighter *Marine Flier,* the beginning of a journey which would take its place one day among the major soporifics of all time. Though neither of them resembled Stevenson's immortal characters in any way—in fact, they looked a good deal more like a couple of indigent process servers or heroin peddlers—the parallel could not be denied. For they too were freckled and they too were undertaking a voyage fraught with high adventure and peril to their expense account. Small wonder that the little knot of bronzed mariners clustered around the stringpiece should have stared after them with the respect men who have wandered into far places accord their own kind, and then have paid

them the highest tribute they knew, that of silently spitting on the sidewalk. It was a picture no artist could paint—least of all, Hirschfeld.

Inside the great echoing shed all was noise and confusion; gangs of stevedores frantically unloaded last-minute cargo from trailers, trucks piled with barrels and cartons scuttled about, perspiring cab-drivers transferred trunks, corded boxes, and bicycles to conveyors. Alongside the pier, her decks swarming with riggers and carpenters, the *Marine Flier* lay low in the water, her seven hatches still receiving goods consigned to China, the Straits Settlements, and India. A dozen huge Samson booms, ten of them amidships, one each at bow and stern, ceaselessly swung bales and packing cases inboard. On the port side of the well deck, a crew of riggers was making fast a giant UNRRA crate of generators destined for Shanghai; on the starboard, carpenters were busily securing innumerable carboys of nitric, hydrochloric, and sulphuric acid for Colombo. Every available foot of deck space was stacked with oil drums, machinery, and galvanized pipe; immediately behind the after house, several longshoremen deftly lashed down an automobile, swathing it in tarpaulins and bracing its wheels with chocks.

It was a scene of activity calculated to inspire even the most torpid, and, eager to swell the total effort, I moved buoyantly from group to group, lightening the burden of one with a rousing sea chantey, regaling a second with a side-splitting anecdote, executing a nimble hornpipe or jig to revive the flagging spirits of a third. In a few moments, scowls had turned to smiles, men who had been at daggers drawn were exchanging 'baccy and teaching each other how to do scrimshaw work, and the feeling was general that my quick-witted tact had forestalled a serious disaffection which might have spread to the entire dockside. Indeed, company officials, who had rushed to the harbor at the first threat of tension, assured me that my trifling intervention had done more to promote harmony in the merchant marine than fifty years of arbitration, and that henceforward capital and labor, their hatchets buried, would march shoulder to shoulder and hand in hand into a new era of mutual understanding, amity, and prosperity. No doubt this was an exaggeration engendered by their profound gratitude, but it was none-theless gratifying; and rejoining Hirschfeld, who had been standing by tapping his foot impatiently, we set off to install ourselves in our cabin.

By a stroke of good fortune, the passenger scheduled to bunk with us had dropped dead the day before, leaving us in comparative comfort. Most of the other passengers were lodged three in a cabin with splendid disregard for their background and personalities. The room next to ours, for example, was shared by a sluggish cotton converter from Philadelphia, a gaunt Jesuit missionary, and a small, fibrous mining engineer. The cotton man turned a beautiful shade of hunter's green directly he boarded the boat and retired groaning to his pillow. The missionary and the engineer, fellow-alumni of the Chapei prison camp, engaged from the outset in a heated and interminable argument about their experiences, each plainly infer-ring the other was a liar. The trio in the other cabin was no less diverse. Tooker, a toothless leprechaun who represented an Amer-ican canned-goods firm in Shanghai, devoted himself largely to special research involving bourbon, rarely emerging even for meals. Linklater and Cropsey, his cabin mates, were also collector's items. The former, a fattish, corpse-like citizen with the benign twinkle of a water moccasin, quickly put every man's hand against him by revealing that he was the ranking mortician of Hong Kong. Cropsey, whose protuberant frog eyes hinted at an obscure thyroid maladjustment deep in his blubber, was a minor insurance official somewhere east of Suez. He spoke with the measured profundity of the true bureaucrat; his most casual opinion was deeply pondered and deliberate, a weighty pronouncement handed down from Sinai. These, together with a Madame Chai, wife of an official in the Chinese Nationalist Government, and her eleven-year-old son, comprised our brave little company outward bound for Chinwang-tao, Shanghai, Hong Kong, and Singapore.

The first couple of days out of the Golden Gate were uneventful. I spent them stretched out in the lower tier of my double berth, gritting my teeth to prevent my tongue from escaping and making a minute study of the plywood ceiling above me. Approximately

Lazy days on the poop: the mortician, the missionary, and S. J.

every fifteen seconds, the *Marine Flier* rose with the speed of an express elevator, shivered deliciously, and lurched steeply forward into the trough. As it reached the bottom of the curve, all the bureau drawers flew out, the locker doors opened, suitcases slid halfway out of the top bunk, and our toilet articles teetered toward the washbowl. The moment the ship began its ascent, the process reversed; with a salvo like the bombardment of Port Arthur, drawers and doors banged shut, suitcases smashed into the wall, and bottles splintered the shaving mirror. It was pikestaff-plain and Doomsday-certain to me, a deep-water sailor since boyhood, that the *Marine Flier* was little more than a cheesebox on a raft and would momentarily founder with all hands. Even the veriest landlubber could perceive that the man whose duty it was to drive the ship—the chauffeur or the motorman or whatever you call him—was behaving with the grossest sort of negligence; more than likely he was asleep at the tiller or tickling the waitress, abandoning the craft to any caprice of wind or wave. But Hirschfeld, who had an answer to everything, irritatingly persisted in minimizing the gravity of our plight.

"It's only the Japan Current," he said perfunctorily. "Every ship to the Orient has to pass through the Japan Current." Japan Current indeed; as if dereliction of duty deserving of a court-martial, aboard a mere cockleshell with one measly funnel, in the worst typhoon in the history of navigation, could be fobbed off with a few glib words about a current. The man's fatuity made my blood boil.

During this trying period, when my every faculty was needed to worry about the proper conduct of the ship, I ate frugally if at all, contenting myself with a cup of thin broth or soda cracker taken betimes; whereas Hirschfeld, with the stolidity of the true peasant, outdid himself in gluttony. Bread by the bushel basket, whole beeves, firkins of butter, and hogsheads of jam vanished down his maw; his arrival at table spread consternation in the galley. He lived only for the ship's bell summoning us to meals; twice he deliberately tripped up Jeffrey Chai, the little Chinese boy, to get the first helping. At last a deputation of our fellow-passengers, hardly more than skin and bones, waited on me and begged my intercession. They pointed out what was long since apparent, that if Hirschfeld prolonged his outrageous behavior, the larder would be clean long before we crossed the International Date Line. The crisis was partially solved by chaining Hirschfeld's leg to his bunk every other meal. The resulting howls and execrations penetrated to the bowels of the vessel: so much so that a deputation of sailors waited on me and begged me to use any means, short of slitting my friend's gullet, to still his dreadful clamor. In the end, I drew on my fairly extensive pre-medical experience and introduced 2.75 gr. of cyclopropane into his matutinal oatmeal, an expedient which

37

kept him in a drowsy, half-animal state most of the day and allowed the rest of us to latch on to a few groceries.

As soon as the advent of a calm sea and favoring winds removed the crushing weight of responsibility from my shoulders and I could again delegate authority to subordinates, I hastened to acquaint myself with the ship's officers and cargo. My knowledge of life on the bridge had been derived from the pages of William McFee and Guy Gilpatric, and I was prepared for weather-beaten, blustering old salts and thorny, iconoclastic Scotch engineers. I looked in vain for them aboard the *Marine Flier.* The relative youth of her officers—her skipper was thirty-two, the first mate thirty-four, and the chief engineer a decrepit thirty—concealed a surprising amount of efficiency and good sense. They were men of taste and a high order of technical skill, refreshingly devoid of heroics or bombast, considerate and socially attractive. The men they commanded were also as far removed from the stock conception of merchant seamen as one could imagine; they had little in common with the alcoholic, improvident sailor of popular fiction and the movies. Many of them were well-schooled and the majority had served with distinction in the war. Through their specialized unions, which sought constantly to improve their status, they had achieved decent living conditions and wages, and, equally important, a sense of self-respect. I could not help feeling that if this ship was any index, there must be a very healthy spirit abroad in the American steamboat business.

The handful of passengers in the after house, of course, was purely incidental to the cargo, worth by rough estimate about a million and a half dollars. It embraced everything imaginable, from shoe polish to bank notes, from steel girders to malted milk. There were, to list only a few items, phonograph records, sardines, jeeps, canned abalone, steam hammers, pencils, bulldozers, haberdashery, beer, railroad ties, telephones, clothespins, aircraft tires, after-shave lotion, quicklime, truck bodies, powdered milk, steel safes, quicksilver, electric ranges, newsprint, resin, plate glass, and depilatories. One of the more curious bits of miscellany was the eleven barrels of ginger which had been spurned by the American

Well deck of the Marine Flier

palate and was now returning in a crestfallen mood to Hong Kong. In the specie tank on the boat deck aft reposed a hundred and sixty cases of Portuguese brandy speeding to the United States consulates in Tientsin and Shanghai; in Number 3 hatch amidships lay two Chinese cadavers, snugly flanked by mouthwash, desk calendars, insect bombs, and movie film. Day by day, at an average speed of fifteen knots, this vast and terrifying hash stored up by some insane magpie crept steadily along the thirty-first parallel to further aggravate the problems of an already chaotic continent.

And now there befell me an incident so grievous that it requires every bit of fortitude I can muster to set it down: the loss of a friend grown dear to me through myriad trials and tribulations, a mainstay in joy and sorrow, the very breath of life itself—my bank roll. The tragedy took place the evening of our seventeenth day, a scant twelve hours before reaching Chinwangtao. Shortly after dinner, I was seated in the smoking room, drawing on an excellent Larranaga and immersed in a fascinating article on Norwegian rainfall in the *National Geographic*. The saloon was a blaze of lights and gaiety; a single forty-watt electric bulb shed its rays over a cutthroat bridge game involving Linklater, Cropsey, Hirschfeld, and the purser, while at a near-by table the missionary bent his head attentively over a photographic reportage in *Pic* by Marie (The Body) MacDonald on the future of the female bust. The card-players had solicited me to join their party, but I remembered my mother's injunction never to fall in with plausible strangers on ocean greyhounds and declined. Just as I was contemplating a bit of shut-eye, the Chinese boy approached. He bore in his palm two unusual amulets of ivory, cube-shaped and speckled with precious stones.

"Why, what are those, Jeffrey?" I inquired, patting the little fellow's head. He explained that they were *su dzai*, an ancient Chinese game of ritualistic origin played on a blanket, in which the contestants wagered on various numerical combinations formed by the amulets. More to divert him than through any vital interest in the game, I consented to play, and we withdrew to a secluded spot behind the ventilators. Extracting from his pinafore an ancient

A cultural evening with the engineer and the first mate of the Marine Flier

Chinese wad which would have choked a horse of the Ming Dynasty, Jeffrey bade me fade him. I complied, and cupping the amulets in his chubby fist, he spun them out smartly.

"*Shau hai dze yau yi saung hai dze!*" he entreated hoarsely.

"How would you translate that, Jeffrey?" I inquired.

"It's an old Shintoist prayer," he replied. "It means 'Baby needs a new pair of shoes.'" The invocation evidently exerted a certain amount of influence over the cubes, because they came up seven a dozen times in a row. The odd thing was that whenever I rolled them, the devilish things behaved in the most perverse fashion. Again and again I tried to breathe fire into them, whispered cunning endearments to them, but it was useless; in the hands of the infidel they produced nothing but deuces and boxcars. The ship's bell was striking midnight as I tore the last American Express check out of my entrails and handed it to Jeffrey.

"There you are, you little swindler," I said bitterly, "and the next time you use loaded dice on a man four times your age, wipe that ugly smirk off your face."

"Thanks, sucker," he said, stowing the check in a money-belt the size of an inner tube. "You know, we Chinese have an old proverb—"

"So do we Yankees," I cut him short. "It runs, 'A fool and his money are soon parted.' Well, *geh in dr'erd*, old man."

"How would you translate that, Mr. Perelman?" he asked.

"I wouldn't," I snapped, turning on my heel. At least, I had one consolation. He may have had my last dollar, but I had had the last word. I mounted the companionway and, picking my way across the cluttered deck, leaned on the rail and stared off through the darkness. A hundred miles distant, across the gently undulating Yellow Sea, waited Asia, inscrutable, brooding. I was starting with a clean slate; could China say the same? That was the question. What would be the answer?

4

The Flowery Kingdom

AN EARLY morning mist, periodically illuminated by the feeble rays of a wintry sun, shrouded the harbor of Chinwangtao as I thrust my head through our porthole on the *Marine Flier* and stared drowsily about me. All I could discern of fabled Cathay was a sullen range of hills disturbingly similar to those we had left behind in Southern California. Into a mind befogged with sleep there gradually crept a dark, hobgoblin suspicion. Suppose that through some error of navigation, some ghastly official blunder, we had overshot Asia and for the past three weeks had been floundering in a vast, idiotic circle around the Pacific. After all, stranger things had happened in the annals of the sea—the celebrated riddle of the *Mary Celeste*, the mysterious disappearance of the Danish training-ship *Kobenhavn*, the enigma of the *Waratah*. I sank down on the edge of the bunk and, head in hands, weighed the evidence. Yes, there was no doubt of it: the captain had made a serious miscalculation in his charts. Instead of pocketing his pride and availing himself of my superior seamanship to get him out of his pickle, he had manifestly preferred to brazen it out. His manner the past few days, now that I reconsidered it, had been extremely evasive; he had slunk past me deliberately avoiding my eye, fearful lest an unguarded word or gesture betray him. If this were indeed Southern California, the captain's intent became only too clear: he was planning to steam straight for Hollywood and drop anchor at Grauman's Chinese, hoping to fob it off on us as the Temple of the Thousand Sleeping Buddhas. There was not a moment to be lost; unless the man's duplicity was unmasked within the hour, our global junket stood in danger of being knocked into a cocked hat. Crossing with a bound to Hirschfeld, my *fidus Achates*, who lay snoring bestially in his bunk, I shook him into consciousness.

"What is it? What's the matter?" the poor fellow cried out, leaping up with his usual faulty co-ordination and inflicting a small gash on his noggin as it struck the upper bunk. I explained our predicament, but his ignorance of matters maritime was abysmal and I could see he only half understood. Wearying of his dramatic groans and fumbling attempts to stanch the blood with a towel (the injury was petty and ceased bleeding long before nightfall), I went forward to reconnoiter and evolve a plan of action.

My fears, luckily, were unfounded; the first thing I beheld was a couple of junks leisurely standing into the harbor and a pilot tug flying the Chinese flag. Just ahead of us was the silvery line of a breakwater and beyond it the cluster of buildings which marked the Kai Lan Mining Administration, the British coal concession controlling the port. By midmorning, our customs and quarantine inspection completed, the ship edged cautiously into her berth beside a dingy, soot-blackened pier striped with railroad tracks. The coolies awaiting us on the dock were decked out in what was unquestionably the most fantastic collection of rags ever assembled anywhere to ward off the weather. A good half possessed no single garment worthy of the name (that is, worthy of the name of garment); the rest wore mangy fur-lined hats or beanies and long, shapeless coats that trailed handfuls of cotton wadding, looped about with odds and ends of canvas and burlap. Their faces were markedly Mongol, and our first impression of them, *en masse* under a gray, lowering sky, was hardly reassuring. I for one would not have been excessively surprised to see Genghis Khan himself appear, flourishing a yataghan, and begin carving a new empire out of the *Marine Flier*. This judgment, however, shortly proved premature. The stevedores were amicable, even jolly; they greeted us warmly, indulged in a good deal of light-hearted banter, and altogether behaved with much more gusto and spirit than hungry people have any right to display. They were particularly awed by Hirschfeld's beard, and expressed their belief to our Jesuit fellow-passenger, who spoke Chinese, that he must be a renowned sage. It would have been shattering to the illusions of these simple folk, not to say disloyal to my friend, to reveal that he could barely read or write, and I prudently kept silence. Hirschfeld, of course, made the most of their homage; he strutted about, stroked his beard portentously, puckered his brow into a frown, moved his lips as though framing some momentous apothegm, and generally ·managed to create a pitiable travesty of a man deep in thought.

The only Occidental visible in the shifting crowd was a vinegary, tight-lipped Englishman in flannels and elegant brown suède shoes, who eyed the ship and everyone aboard her with ill-concealed disfavor. It was obvious that to our British cousin the arrival of the *Marine Flier* was no signal to fling his beret into the air. The junior mate, leaning beside us on the docking bridge, watched him with foreboding. "Trouble," he predicted gloomily. It appeared that we had called at Chinwangtao, a port rarely included in the freight schedule, to discharge twenty-five hundred tons of girdles (at least, it sounded like that; the engine-room bell was clanging and he may have said girders). Whatever they were, they lay well down in the hatches, and piled on top of them were quantities of miscellaneous cargo destined for Shanghai. This overstow would have to be removed, stored in godowns, or warehouses, while the girdles were being unloaded, and subsequently replaced. It was an expensive and tedious process, and if, he observed darkly, the port had no godown facilities, we would be in a pretty fix.

"What would we do then?"

"Search me, Buster," he shrugged. "The inside of this here vessel is just one big grab-bag." I left him staring balefully at the wharf, and rounding up Hirschfeld, the Jesuit father, and the Philadelphia cotton converter, I proposed a stroll into the town. At the foot of the gangplank, the Englishman accosted us.

"I shouldn't go up there if I were you."

"We were just going to stretch our legs."

"You may get your necks stretched." He uttered a short, mirth-

The only Occidental visible in the shifting crowd was a vinegary, tight-lipped Englishman in flannels and elegant suède shoes

less laugh. "There's the very devil to pay. The whole town's under martial law. The Communists are only five miles away. They've been blowing up the tracks between here and Tientsin every other night." Assuming a formidable Russian accent, Hirschfeld informed him that we were American Communist agents sent to bolster the morale of our Red comrades and that we would stick at nothing to help drive the parasites out of China, leaving no question in his voice whom he meant. The Englishman's lip curled. Our political sympathies were our own affair, he said, but he could tell us that if we ventured into Chinwangtao, he could not personally be responsible for our safety. We exchanged smiles tipped with the most malignant hatred and set off.

Our route into town lay across a tangle of railroad tracks skirting the bay; the wind was bitter and the scenery reminiscent of the less attractive suburbs of Carteret, New Jersey. Presently we came out upon a cement highway bordered by dusty, leafless saplings, along which hurried hordes of rather tense Chinese. Dispersed along the road at intervals were brick pillboxes manned by fifteen-year-old soldiers in heavily padded blue uniforms, exhibiting fixed bayonets with some ostentation. Before very long, a party of rickshaw men waylaid us. One of them, not to be put off by our repeated plea that we wanted to walk, scampered beside me. He offered to lead me to a house of tolerance, where, he implied, delights never imagined by Havelock Ellis and Krafft-Ebing might be viewed at moderate cost. I regretfully declined. He pondered a second, then withdrew from his singlet a packet of photographs which I gathered to be sporting scenes. I rarely hunt or fish, and I told him so. Undeterred, he inquired whether I wished to dally with his sister. I assured him I had every regard for her, but I had sworn to remain celibate until Ireland assumes its rightful place in the comity of nations. I was sorry when he finally fell astern and vanished up an alley. He was an engaging rogue, and though he would have cheerfully slit my windpipe for a shiny red apple, it had been fun knowing him.

A veritable fusillade of smells, compounded of the pungent odors of deep fat, shark's fin, sandalwood, and open drains, now bombarded our nostrils and we found ourselves in the thriving hamlet of Chinwangtao. Every sort of object imaginable was being offered by street hawkers—basketwork, noodles, poodles, hardware, leeches, breeches, peaches, watermelon seeds, roots, boots, flutes, coats, shoats, stoats, even early vintage phonograph records. In a pile of the latter, I discovered a fairly well-preserved copy of that classical minstrelsy, "Cohen on the Telephone," but the moment the merchant sensed he was dealing with an American, the price shot up to three cents and I thought better of it. A band of ten or fifteen urchins trooped at our heels constantly, wiping their noses freely on our sleeves and demanding cumshaw. Children, I may as well confess it, are my weakness; I distributed a few worn gold pieces which were of no further use to me and earned their undying gratitude. It is pathetic that trinkets like these, utterly without value in the States, should be sought after so eagerly throughout the rest of the world. The prospective traveler who seeks an advantageous rate of exchange will do far better to fill his trunks with gold pieces than the oft-heralded nylons, chewing gum, and cigarettes.*

Marster like real art picture nineteen poses?

It was almost lunchtime when we started back toward the ship, each in his individual rickshaw. I experienced what I am told is the customary sense of embarrassment at having a fellow-creature act as one's beast of burden, but mine was such a wiry specimen, weighing as he did well over eighty pounds and amaz-

* This was written in the early spring of 1947. The situation may have altered since, of course.—*Author's note.*

ingly fleet for a man of sixty with tuberculosis, that I quickly over-came my compunctions. Besides, as your old China hand loves to observe, if everybody stopped riding in rickshaws through humani-tarian scruples, their pullers would soon starve. It was, therefore, with the fairly cocky feeling I had done my bit to avert a possible famine that I dismounted and gave my boy his eleven cents. He must have appreciated my altruistic motives, for the instant he ceased coughing and sponged the perspiration from his face, he was profuse in his thanks.

We were treading gingerly through the maze of the freight yards when the faint blast of a steamer whistle echoed from the direction of the port. We stood momentarily rooted to the spot, and then, like a cork blown out of a bottle, the Jesuit father took off. I will stake my wig that, paced by Father Houlihan, the four of us broke every hurdle record in the last fifty years. It was a gallant try but foredoomed to failure. By the time we reached the pierhead, tongues lolling out of our mouths, the *Marine Flier* was beyond the breakwater and fading fast. The sole person in sight was our English milord, teetering on his heels and richly enjoying our dis-may. "I warned you," he chuckled. Slowly, and savoring each word, he revealed that since there was no storage space for the overstow, our ship had left for Shanghai without unloading. It was a bleak prospect: all our passports, luggage, and funds slipping over the horizon, a civil war five miles away, and no American consul this side of Peiping. Ultimately, the Englishman finished draining his cup of triumph and relented. A tug was summoned and we were taken aboard ingloriously, in a heaving sea, amid the jeers and cat-calls of the other passengers. One of them was so unsporting as to snap a photograph of me creeping on my hands and knees across the gangplank, which he later showed around to much raucous laughter. To tell the truth, I found the levity a trifle mechanical, but I joined in good-naturedly, ever ready to guffaw over the dis-comfiture of another human being.

Two mornings later, we steamed slowly up the muddy mouth of the Yangtze past the Woosung Forts and began threading our way

The tender which bore us to the Bund had no allotted slip or jetty; it merely tied up in slapdash fashion against five other boats

through the sixteen miles of river traffic that separated us from our anchorage. How the pilot ever managed to maneuver the ship to her berth without running down a single sampan I do not profess to know; a dozen times it looked like Judgment Day for entire families of Chinese, but grandmother and three-year-old alike would throw themselves on the sweep and pump hysterically until the craft veered out of our path. Freighters from every conceivable port in the world—Oslo, Honduras, Liverpool, Veracruz, Amsterdam —were being lightered in midstream, further adding to the hazard. At last, around a bend of the Whangpoo, Shanghai came into sight and we slid along the Bund, fronted by hotels and office buildings, up to the Dollar docks on the Pootung side.

A charming bit of intelligence greeted us. The bowlines were scarcely secured before word arrived that in three days we were to head back to Chinwangtao and discharge the girdles after all. A pall descended on the ship; Hirschfeld and I sat drearily in the deserted smoking room, wondering whether to transfer to another ship, or stay ashore until the *Flier* returned, or just hang ourselves from the nearest yardarm. We probably would have done the last had not the captain anticipated us and hid it in a locker. Eventually we decided to spend a night or two in Shanghai and see what diversions it offered. All the way across the Pacific there had been rumors of exquisitely complaisant White Russian countesses and unimaginable sins. Neither of us smoked opium, but we had no objection to learning. We thought we might even pick up a priceless bit of jade. We were in a mood for adventure. We got it.

We received the first installment before we even set foot on the levee. The tender which bore us to the Bund had no allotted slip or jetty; it merely tied up in slapdash fashion against five other boats each moored to the one adjoining it, and the passengers swarmed over the lot like ants over a sugar bowl. In effect, what you had was a Bronx subway rush with water jumps. One moment I was braced against a stanchion gaping at the skyline; the next, I was caught up in a swirl of coolies and shot forward down into a barge full of stones. I clawed my way across it, sprang down a dark companionway, stumbled over three citizens stuffing themselves with bean curd, and landed in a perilously tossing sampan. As I straightened up to catch my breath, the second wave hit me. I saw Hirschfeld go past, flailing and kicking, his beard high in the air. "Hirschfeld!" I screamed piteously, "*Tovarisch!*" He paid me no attention; he had other fish to fry. I lowered my head like a bull and, with two Cantonese encircling me, did a line plunge. I reached terra firma a broken man, my collar in shreds, eyeglasses twisted, streaming with perspiration. Hirschfeld was nursing a wrenched knee, having slipped and fallen between two boats in the melee. He had a bloody nose and had lost a shoe, but otherwise he was as fit as a fiddle.

To regain some measure of poise, we proceeded to the Cathay Hotel, reputedly Shanghai's finest, and had a drink apiece. The bill came to $39,000 Chinese National Currency—about $3.36—and we left a tip of $5000, or 41 cents. The exchange rate at the moment was twelve thousand Chinese dollars to the American one, and prices had more or less kept abreast. Our room, for instance, was $120,000 a day—slightly over ten dollars—and our breakfast $14,000. The real drawback, though, was the complete lack of any form of heat. A ton of coal cost three hundred U. S. dollars—in any case, a purely academic consideration at the Cathay, as the Japanese had stripped it of radiators and boilers. That night will linger in my memory as one of the most agonizing I have ever endured. Our teeth chattered so loudly that several Americans resident there phoned the Embassy to report gunfire. Just to indicate how cold it was, I left a tumbler of water at my bedside and when I woke up, it was gone. Hirschfeld had drunk it and also had eaten the glass. That was one cold night.

The following day we embarked on a shopping tour of the antique bazaars in the Kwantung Road, charmed at every turn by the indescribable wealth of imagination the Chinese lavish on their art. Surrounded by so much beauty, it was difficult to determine what to choose; Hirschfeld finally settled on an imitation cloisonné cigarette stand complete with match receptacle and ash-trays, and I bought three ivory back-scratchers you could not duplicate in San Francisco for less than a quarter. About midafternoon we traced

The bad news: a lodging for the night in Shanghai

CATHAY HOTEL

SHANGHAI

Room No. 7/24/41

M Mr. S.J. Perelman & Mr. A. Hirschfeld

martz

	8	9	$	$	$	$	$	$
		$126,000-						
Apartments	$120,000-							
Inclusive Terms								
Breakfast								
Luncheon								
Tea								
Dinner								
Special Orders	$14,000-							
Supper								
Tea, Coffee and Milk								
Fruit &c.								
& Cigarettes								
In Luncheon								
Tea								
Restaurant Dinner								
Supper								
Telephone								
Laundry								
Valet Service								
Newspapers								
Motors								
Baggage								
Flowers								
Paid Out:—								
Service Charge	Tax $6,000- 2/00-							
Carried forward	$126,000- $142/00 ————							
Less Cash Paid								
Less Allowances								

Accounts are due the day they are rendered. Cheques cannot be accepted

NO RECEIPT RECOGNIZED UNLESS ON THE COMPANY'S OFFICIAL FORM

PLEASE LEAVE YOUR FORWARDING ADDRESS

KINDLY VERIFY YOUR RECEIPT WITH THE TOTAL AMOUNT OF THIS STATEMENT

ALL STATEMENTS MUST BE NUMBERED

our steps to the American Club, a pleasant establishment in Foochow Road made doubly delightful by the circumstance that it had the only heated bar in town. Five whiskey sours drove the chill from our bones, and we decided to have a drink. There then ensued a hazy interval during which I seem to recall the sound of a cupful of poker dice being thrown repeatedly against a board and a playful attempt on my part to comb Hirschfeld's beard with a back-scratcher. From time to time strange faces swam into my field of vision; I remember a laborious, protracted recital by an UNRRA official of his difficulties in persuading the Chinese to eat canned peaches, but part of it was being given in Russian and some men were accompanying him on balalaikas. It suddenly grew much colder and I found myself in a very dim night club, teaching an exophthalmic Hungarian girl the Cubanola glide. The next morning I felt remarkably listless and there was an outbreak of beef Stroganoff on my tie as though I were coming down with a fever, but these symptoms soon passed, and by noon I was able to keep down a little clear broth made of Angostura, lemon peel, and bourbon.

What with the penetrating cold and the cost of living in Shanghai, it seemed on the whole inadvisable to tarry, and folding our hands submissively we journeyed north once more to Chinwangtao on the *Flier*. It took four interminable days to get rid of our cargo; my companion mooned in the cabin buffing his nails and I made a short excursion to Shanhaikwan to see the Great Wall. The Great Wall can also be seen facing page 556 of the Encyclopaedia Britannica by simply stretching your hand toward the bookcase, though the chances of picking up a flea are very much smaller. Shanhaikwan, it is interesting to note, has the smallest fleas in China; they are much prized by collectors, but I was fortunate enough to secure three or four fine specimens. As the Chinese Government strictly forbids their export, I had to smuggle them out in my clothing, but I managed to get them through to Singapore safe and sound.

Shanghai once more, and this time it was the twenty-eighth of March, the end of the first week of spring. All through it we had lain alongside the wharf, the Plimsoll line rising hourly higher as ton after ton of goods went over the side. Across the river, in the barren fields, the trees had begun to show a cloudy green nimbus; the sun was hot, and in the sampans drifting downstream groups of children were playing jacks. I lounged on the boat deck and thought of the Pennsylvania countryside, of the forsythia primrose-yellow against the barn, the Judas tree bursting into bloom, the swollen creek tumbling through the pasture. I asked myself what I was doing ten thousand miles from home, on what obscure quest I had come, and I could find no answer. Perhaps Thoreau knew; he knew everything. I went into my cabin and got out *Walden*. There it was, in that always concise and astringent prose, the *vade mecum* for every wanderer:

"It is not worth the while to go round the world to count the cats in Zanzibar. Yet do this even till you can do better, and you may perhaps find some 'Symmes' Hole' by which to get at the inside at last. England and France, Spain and Portugal, Gold Coast and Slave Coast, all front on this private sea; but no bark from them has ventured out of sight of land, though it is without doubt the direct way to India. If you would learn to speak all tongues and conform to the customs of all nations, if you would travel farther than all travellers, be naturalized in all climes, and cause the Sphinx to dash her head against a stone, even obey the precept of the old philosopher, and Explore thyself. Herein are demanded the eye and the nerve. Only the defeated and deserters go to the wars, cowards that run away and enlist. Start now on that farthest western way, which does not pause at the Mississippi or the Pacific, nor conduct toward a worn-out China or Japan, but leads on direct, a tangent to this sphere, summer and winter, day and night, sun down, moon down, and at last earth down too."

5

Carry Me Back to Old Pastrami

PRECISELY six weeks from the raw midwinter evening on which the S.S. *Marine Flier* had cleared the Golden Gate for the Chinese ports and Singapore, a pair of passengers in rumpled seersucker and shirts that gave every evidence of having laundered themselves teetered down the accommodation ladder and landed unsteadily on the dockside at Kowloon. Across the bay, at the base of a volcanic peak studded with opulent villas, lay huddled the historic crown colony of Hong Kong, Far Eastern bastion of Britain's thin red line of empire. The two American *Wandervogels* contemplating the panorama before them were a striking sight—the prognathous jaw of Perelman smoothly flowing into a skull resembling that of Cro-Magnon Man, Hirschfeld's cunning ferret eyes gleaming above his unkempt tangle of beard, and beyond, in the quickening dusk, the mighty colonial outpost immortalized by Hoagy Carmichael in his rondeau of the very unfortunate Chinaman. For a full minute they paused lost in admiration of this city hewn from the living rock, so much a symbol of the indomitable British character, and then Hirschfeld gave vent to a long-drawn sigh.

"You know what I'd do if that were mine?" he asked. I turned toward him impulsively, knowing that in the wellsprings of his heart there dwelt a true libertarian, a man flash-quick and whippet-fast to sympathize with the oppressed and downtrodden. I was not disappointed; when he spoke again, it was in a voice vibrant with feeling: "I'd trade it all for a hot pastrami sandwich." The homely phrase, freighted with nostalgia, found my Achilles' heel; on the instant all the secret pent-up longing of weeks burst forth and we wept uncontrollably on each other's shoulders, shedding hot salt pastrami tears. I believe that had there been a branch of Lindy's within forty miles of Hong Kong that night, we would have cheerfully crept there on our hands and knees. It was the beginning of a homesickness which, as the trip progressed, took on the proportions of an obsession; time and again, in such unlikely places as the Temple of the Emerald Buddha and the ruins of Fatehpur Sikri, a vision of strawberry cheesecake would swim before us, taunting us almost to the brink of madness.

To the naked eye, and ours were reasonably nude as we ventured up the central avenue of Kowloon, Hong Kong's principal suburb was indistinguishable from Asbury Park out of season. There were the same depressingly uniform rows of yellow stucco apartments, the same flyblown stationery stores featuring outdated copies of *Peek* and *Leer*, the same curio shops full of sleazy kimonos, brass daggers, incense burners, and souvenir pillows engraved with the Chinese equivalent of "Fir Yew I Pine and Balsam Too." At the Kowloon Hotel we drank warm Danish beer under the whirling overhead fans and eavesdropped on a quartet of Royal Marine Commandos boasting about their amatory exploits. For a while we sat enthralled at the lushness of their profanity and their dauntless ability to interthread every third word with one of the breezier copulative verbs, but soon ennui supervened and we set off listlessly for the ship. Suddenly, without any warning, adventure appeared in the person of a brisk young American naval intelligence officer. Lieutenant Wilson, it developed, had heard on the grapevine that Hirschfeld and I were footloose in Asia; he was on his way to an audience with Bao Dai, the deposed Emperor of Annam in Indo-China, and wondered if we cared to accompany him. The invitation could not have been more beautifully timed, for, curiously enough, I had just finished observing to Hirschfeld that I could not imagine balmier weather for meeting deposed Annamite emperors. It was one of those creepy coincidences which occur in actual life, but which, when the novelist employs them, sound so implausible.

Riding over to Hong Kong on the ferry, we gleaned a few vital

statistics about Bao Dai. He had belonged to possibly the oldest
ruling family in the world, was thirty-three years old, was rumored
to have thirty-three children, and was regarded as semi-divine by
his people. His palace at Hué, before its destruction by the Viet-
namese, was reported to have been of a magnificence unparalleled
even in the imagination of Darryl Zanuck. For the past sixteen
months of his exile, while waiting hopefully for the French to
restore him to his throne, he had been living in Hong Kong, at-
tending at least one movie daily and spending his evenings at a
taxi dance hall. Other than that, Wilson knew nothing. He had never
met the former monarch personally, but poolroom gossip had it that
he was a sweet, wholesome kid.

The pleasure dome where His Majesty frolicked nightly turned
out to be a somewhat sedater version of Broadway's Roseland; ten
or twelve British and Eurasian couples were foxtrotting grimly to
"I Found a Roach in the Devil's Garden," played with deafening
incompetence by sixteen impassive Chinese. Bao Dai was seated
in a snug alcove surrounded by several hostesses whose skinny necks
and high-pitched avian cackle lent them more than a passing resemblance to a flock of spring fryers. The royal exile, a short,
slippery-looking customer rather on the pudgy side and freshly
dipped in Crisco, wore a fixed, oily grin that was vaguely reptilian.
Since he spoke almost no English, the interview was necessarily
limited to pidgin and whatever pathetic scraps of French we could
remember from Frazier and Square. To put him at his ease, I
inquired sociably whether the pen of his uncle was in the garden.
Apparently the query was fraught with delicate political implications involving the conflict in Indo-China, for he shrugged evasively
and buried his nose in his whiskey-and-soda.

"Why don't you try him on the movies?" suggested Lieutenant
Wilson, gently disentangling the fingers of a hostess from the
wallet in his hip pocket. The notion seemed a fertile one; a little
adroit questioning revealed that His Highness's favorite screen
actress was Jeanette MacDonald. Here indeed was a common bond;
I disclosed that at a distant epoch of my life, under the lash of
hunger, I had helped contrive the *mise en scène* for one of her

H.R.H. the Ex-Emperor of Annam
and a couple of China Chicks

films, a pestilence called *Sweethearts*. Bao Dai was immediately enchanted. Could I divulge any little personality secrets, any charming traits or whimsies to aid him toward a fuller understanding of the noted *vedette*? I told him regretfully that I could not, apart from the fact that she was known colloquially in Hollywood as "The Iron Butterfly" and her co-star as "The Singing Capon"; I had never wittingly exposed myself to her glamour. A thoughtful five-minute silence followed this cultural exchange, ended by the entrance of a small, silky party who was evidently a combination of finger man, public relations counsel, and court chamberlain. He drew me aside and, to the strains of "Milenberg Joys," cleared up what he termed to be several popular misconceptions about the boss. For example, he said, certain elements had been circulating tales that His Highness liked to smoke a little pipe or two. He could brand this as a calumny; His Highness was a serious student of international affairs who kept abreast of all the latest political developments and was deeply interested in economics, sociology, archaeology, paleontology, epistemology, hagiology, and dendrology. Backbiters were also saying that His Highness was frivolous because he went to the movies every afternoon. If he did, it was only in an effort to improve his English. (I tried to ascertain just what His Highness was improving at the Paramount Ballrooms, but all I got was a grunt.) At this juncture, a bone-cracking yawn contorted the regal lineaments, clearly signifying that the audience was over. We shook hands formally all around, paid through the nose for the refreshments and the society of the ladies, and took off, grateful that we had had this rare chance to cement international good-fellowship.

In the two or three days the *Marine Flier* lingered at Hong Kong, we naturally had only the most fleeting opportunity to look around, but what we saw was a welcome contrast to the confusion and grinding poverty of Shanghai. British authority, if unable to house and feed all the homeless, had nevertheless succeeded in establishing a sense of cleanliness and order. Scattered houses still showed where Japanese bombs had fallen, but they were fast being rebuilt and it was obvious the war had receded in people's minds.

The island is a lovely one; the scenery in the vicinity of Repulse Bay and Stanley Village, with its many coves and headlands, is certainly as delightful as any I know. It would have been pleasant to vegetate awhile in the sun and contemplate each other's navels. Hirschfeld, however, was not only self-conscious but had no navel. Perhaps, though, I could get him one; I'd heard you could get almost anything where I was going next—namely, Macao.

It was unthinkable for anyone who had consumed as much pulp fiction as myself to put into Hong Kong without visiting Macao, widely acclaimed as the wickedest city in the East, and I lost no time in making the pilgrimage. Macao, the last remnant of Portuguese glory in China, lies four and a half hours from the crown colony by coastal ferry and is usually mentioned in a furtive whisper after the ladies have left the table. According to Hendrik de Leeuw's *Cities of Sin* and "Rainbow in Blood Alley," a story in a recent issue of *Esquire*, this tiny community is one of the most sinister places on earth; the Casbah in Algiers and the Cannebière in Marseilles are as meetings of the Dorcas Society by comparison. To it, the legend goes, gravitate the cutthroat, gambler, Jezebel, and drug addict when the underworld finally closes its doors; whatever your whim, whether opium, fan-tan, or the sing-song girls, Macao waits to gratify it.

On the basis of an overnight sojourn, I can report that I found the Pearl of the Orient slightly less exciting than a rainy Sunday evening in Rochester. I checked into the Grand Hotel on the Avenida Almeira Ribeiro about nine-thirty in the evening with my pulses playing the *Bolero*, a sheaf of bank notes pinned inside my shirt, and a fever of 102. I was loaded for bear and equipped to cut a wide swath through the night life. Although my enthusiasm had been dampened momentarily by a Portuguese *senhor* on the boat, who informed me that the principal industries were the salting of fish and the manufacture of firecrackers, I figured he was concealing something. After all, a public librarian and licensee in economic and financial law, as his card proclaimed him to be, could not be expected to know the hot spots.

At the Central Hotel, a ramshackle structure advertised as the ultimate in gaiety and chic, I managed to procure at considerable expense one of the worst meals I have ever eaten in my life. It was constructed around a chicken that had accompanied Vasco da Gama on his earliest voyage of exploration; the flesh was in an almost perfect state of petrifaction and the chef, in a palpable effort to tickle my palate, had cunningly skewered it with a hairpin. It was served by three lethargic youths and a couple of equally apathetic teen-age misses in middy blouses, all five of whom moved with the fixed, trancelike rigidity of somnambulists. Fighting off a growing sense of depression, I made my way to the combination gambling casino and cabaret on the roof. My dinner may have been a wash-out, I conceded, but from here in things were going to be strictly E. Phillips Oppenheim—lovely haggard women staking their last franc on the turn of a card, lean satanic operatives with black monocles and impeccable evening clothes, the mingled scent of Nuit d'Amour, Sobranies, and hashish.

The gambling hell, I was a bit taken aback to discover, was a bleak, echoing auditorium of the type favored by Lithuanian glee clubs for their monthly singfests. The half dozen sleepy Chinese girls presiding over the fan-tan tables eyed me with a pronounced lack of interest and returned to their dog-eared movie magazines. Word must have spread, nevertheless, that a red-hot Yankee spend-thrift had entered the premises, because the orchestra in the next room forthwith struck up one of our characteristic popular airs, "Pony Boy." Squaring my shoulders, I entered a murky grillroom such as you might discover in the second-best hotel in Columbia, South Carolina. Here fun was at its maddest; two pairs of Chinese hostesses sporting spectacular gold teeth were dancing torpidly with each other while a few pimply Portuguese sports lay around glassily, fanning themselves and waiting for a coronary thrombosis to put them out of their misery. I had consumed the major portion of a bottle of abominable red wine when the headwaiter came up, chaperoning a fat girl with frizzed hair and a mottled complexion.

"Allow me to present a most beautiful person, Miss Linda Andra-da," he bowed. "She has consented to share your company for a small fee." The beautiful person thereupon ordered a lime smash and we conversed haltingly for an hour about life and letters in Macao. By another of those strange literary coincidences, Miss Andrada's favorite actress also turned out to be Jeanette Mac-Donald, for whom, she confessed archly, she had often been mistaken. I assured her that the resemblance was uncanny and confided that I too had been frequently mistaken for Richard Burbage. Unfortunately, just as our friendship was burgeoning into something that might today be a bitter-sweet memory, the orchestra played a farewell flourish. My vis-à-vis coyly intimated that if I were masterful enough, she might be prevailed upon to show me some rare old Portuguese mezzotints at her flat, but as I could not conceivably have gone there without my duenna, I was forced to decline. We parted with fervent promises to write each other daily and I made off for my hotel through a network of dark alleys. It must have been an off night in Macao, for when I reached my room and undressed, there was not a single haft of a knife protruding from the small of my back. True, the springless Chinese bed I slept on could not compare with my Beautyrest, and I can still taste the toast spread with yak fat I breakfasted on the next morning, but for sheer profligacy, for debauchery like Mother used to make, that evening at the Central will long live in my memory. When I regained the *Marine Flier*, Hirschfeld and the other passengers inevitably insisted on hearing about my experiences, but I merely laid my finger slyly alongside my nose and gave them a knowing wink. If the exploit accomplished nothing else, it raised my prestige in the fo'c'sl. The next morning, as I passed a couple of old sea-dogs splicing rope amidships, I heard one whisper respectfully, "That's the man who spent the night in Macao."

Two days south of Hong Kong, the heat began; awnings appeared on the afterdeck and the fantail, the cabins were loud with the whine of electric fans, and life moved in a slower, lazier rhythm. During the day the metal decks blazed underfoot; there were violent tropical downpours, sunsets that made the reason totter, nights filled with a million stars. The young American matron at our table, returning home to face a difficult divorce, unexpectedly found her-

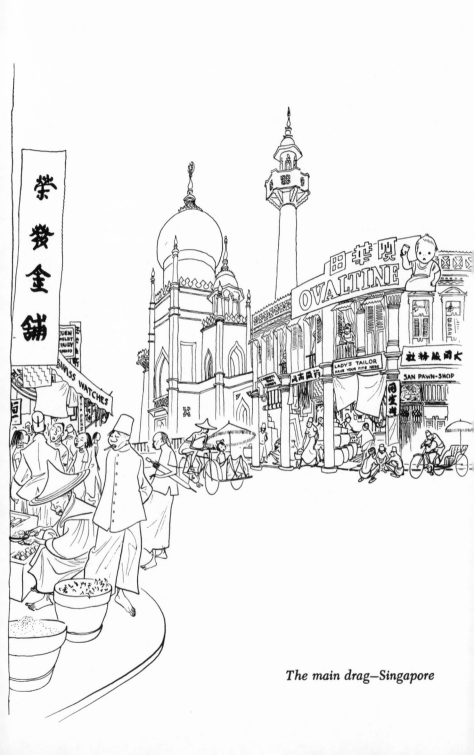

The main drag—Singapore

self the object of furious adoration by the third mate; the deck and engineer cadets dawdled endlessly about her daughter, flexing their muscles and holding long philosophical symposiums about love.

"I think that if a man gives a girl his class ring, why then she oughtn't to date anybody else."

"Yes, but it's not like an *engagement* ring, dope."

"It could be, if he wants it that way. I heard of a girl that was secretly engaged to a man for four years and everybody thought she was just wearing his class ring."

"Did they get married?"

"No, he went back to prep school."

"There you are. If this man was really serious about this girl, he'd have given her a real ring, not a little old *class* ring."

Then, one hot sultry morning, we awoke to the rattle of the anchor chains in the Singapore roadstead and the realization, at once gratifying and oppressive, that we had reached the midway mark of our journey. Seated in the tender pulling away from the *Marine Flier,* our luggage heaped about us, we waved goodbye to officers and crew with a sense of unreality; already they were strangers, phantoms whose identity we would puzzle over in a drawerful of blackened snapshots. The sun was high overhead and merciless by the time we arrived at the Raffles Hotel, and it was good to relax over a gimlet in the cool darkness, even if the celebrated bar did fall short of my preconceptions. I had expected something straight out of Somerset Maugham, paneled in mahogany and full of aquiline-featured cads involved in desperate intrigues with the wives of neighboring planters. What I saw instead was a double row of tables strongly suggestive of a Childs restaurant, flanking a dance floor that cried out for a mother-of-pearl jukebox to complete its utter commonplaceness. The people about us may have been cads, but their skins had been tanned by gin and bitters rather than fierce tropical suns. At noon the room began taking on the aspect of a New Jersey beach hotel; comfortable bourgeois families exchanged condolences about the servant problem and their children slid up and down the dance floor, whooping and pinching each other. It was very disillusioning, and whether it was due to travel fatigue, or the

four gimlets I had taken, or the end of my boyhood dream, it made me want to cry.

That night Hirschfeld and I lay in our mosquito-netted trundle beds in the room we shared with two other birds of passage and listened reverently to the muted pulsebeat of the East. Down the gallery an asthmatic phonograph was scratching out Count Basie's "One O'clock Jump" and next door an Australian woman whimpered for clemency as her liege lord methodically beat the living kapok out of her. Ever and again the snores of our fellow-lodgers rose antiphonally, interspersed with melancholy groans and paraphrases of *Finnegans Wake*. I heard a vicious slap and Hirschfeld's stifled malediction.

"You know," I murmured thoughtfully, "we could have had all this in the Bronx for a five-cent subway ride."

"Sure," agreed Hirschfeld, "but who the hell would believe it?"

6

The Road to Mandalay

THE OLD Vauxhall saloon swung off the macadam road, emitted a tragic, lingering cough evocative of Camille, and, pistons hammering, panted up the long graveled driveway. Ahead of us, through the casuarinas and banana palms, appeared the outlines of a rambling, cream-colored villa—the residence of the Tungku Makhota, His Highness Ismail, Grandfather of the Shrine, Commander of the Most Noble and Exalted Order of St. Michael and St. George, Prince Regent and Heir Apparent of the throne of the Malay state of Johore. Wedged in the rear seat beside me, Hirschfeld cleared his throat nervously, produced a pocket comb for at least the tenth time that morning, and curried his beard, fluffing it out until it frothed like a zabaglione around his chin.

"Do you think I look all right?" he whispered anxiously. It was evident that the strain of our impending visit to the home of the Malay potentate was telling on him; his hand shook and a drop of perspiration glinted on his forehead, almost obscuring it. By contrast, though I say it in no spirit of braggadocio, I was as glacial and reserved as Sumner Welles at a B'nai B'rith picnic. Despite the fact that I had donned two left shoes and an ambassadorial sash that clashed slightly with my khaki shorts, I bore myself with icy *sangfroid* and a determination not to let myself be overawed. From the moment the Regent had signified through a go-between in Singapore that he would be pleased to receive us at luncheon, I had known exactly what attitude I should adopt toward him. Not for me to play the servile toady, the cringing lickspittle; no hangdog caitiff I. I would slap him on the back with easy backwoods familiarity, offer him a chaw of Mail Pouch, and drawl, "Wa'al, pardner, I reckon we folks over yonder don't sot much store by this king stuff, but by vum, I ain't minded to hold it agin ye. I like my vittles plain, my likker straight, and my women purty. I don't rile easy, but when I'm mean, I'm ornery as pizen, an' I kin whup my weight in bobcats. I aim to shoot squar', but if'n you're a wrong Injun—watch out!"

The car screeched to a stop beneath a cement porte-cochere; a pair of Malay guards in smart gray-green uniforms and bare feet sprang to attention, stiffly presenting their carbines. Simultaneously, a plump, dark-skinned gentleman in a purple sports shirt appeared dynamically at the stairhead, surrounded by half a dozen huge Belgian shepherd dogs gamboling in a frenzy about him. "There you are, there you are!" he exclaimed, his manner clearly betraying he had not the foggiest notion of our identity. "Come along now, both of you, come along!" I was just preparing to deliver my homespun salutation when one of the dogs darted between my legs from behind and I was catapulted indoors, straddling the brute in a highly undignified and, indeed, perilous fashion. Had I not had the quick-wittedness to wrap my arms tightly about the dog's neck and gallop until he sank under me, I might easily have dashed out my brains on the terrazzo floor. The hazard I stood in must have escaped the spectators, for the Regent, obviously a man with a primitive sense of humor, burst into howls of mirth, in which Hirschfeld, ever eager to scrape favor with persons of consequence, hastily joined. I pride myself that my sense of the absurd is as keen as the next man's, and goodness knows I relish a joke even at my own expense; but what there was in my plight to provoke screams of laughter, I do not know. Possibly they had never seen a man on a dog before.

Administering a surreptitious kick to the mongrel who had almost cooked my goose, I followed our host through a series of vast bilious chambers crowded with modernique skyscraper furniture and presently fetched up in a room that put the Roxy lounge to shame. Scattered about it in frozen groups suggestive of the waxworks at the Eden Musée sat twelve or fourteen British colonials and their ladies,

*Fashion note:
the slip
that doesn't*

staring frigidly at each other and murmuring "Quaite." Every so
often, one of the more mettlesome would lean forward, suck his
false dentures into position, and whinny, "I say, I do love a bit of
Stilton now and then. It never lets you down." I drained off a cocktail compounded of saddle soap and *crème de cacao* and proceeded
to inspect the objects of virtu housed in glass cases around the walls.
The jade, rose quartz, and ivories would certainly have made any
museum curator swoon with desire; there were porcelains, enamels,
and gold ornaments beyond all value; but what made the collection
particularly noteworthy was the owner's utter catholicity of taste.
Side by side with his most priceless bijoux were gewgaws straight
out of a Sixth Avenue schlock store—worry-birds, lynchee dolls, and
all manner of related bric-a-brac. A plaster cast of an Italian fisher-
boy nibbling a bunch of cherries stood cheek by jowl with a jade
Buddha that must have cost an entire Chinese province; two fabulous Ming vases shared honors with a Mickey Mouse ash-tray from
some Coney Island ski-ball concession. Just as Hirschfeld and I were
examining, with a certain degree of repulsion, a tinted photograph
of the Regent posed before his Mercedes-Benz, which he had caused
to be snipped out and mounted on cardboard like an icon, he buzzed
over to us.

"Well?" he inquired, preening himself with a small jade preening
fork. "What do you think of my collection?"

"So-so, bub," I rejoined carelessly. "I like a couple of those doo-
dads you've got there."

"In other words," purred the Regent, a sinister gleam invading
his eye, "you think the rest of it is junk, eh?" Hirschfeld's blood
froze; he immediately saw visions of us being garrotted in the courtyard, flung into moats boiling with crocodiles. He trod heavily on
my toe to warn me of our danger, but I refused to be deflected.

"Yes, wise guy," I snapped, "a lot of it *is* junk." The prince
chuckled.

"I agree with you," he said mildly, "but I like junk. Wait till you
see what you get for lunch."

He was as good as his word. Never have I eaten tapioca in so
many forms. There was tapioca soup, filet of tapioca, roast vest of

tapioca, tapioca cookies, and a special dessert made of tapioca, bamboo, and shad roe that had been run through a carburetor, dried, and buried under a banyan tree for two years. To further add to my tribulations, I was placed opposite the wife of the Regent, who wore in her corsage a diamond of such matchless water that every time I looked up, its brilliance well-nigh blinded me. Hirschfeld, seated next to her, kept eying it with ill-concealed cupidity. At length, having screwed up his courage, he launched into an elaborate paroxysm of coughing, and using his napkin as a shield, tried to wrench the bauble off the royal balcony, but all he got for his pains was a stinging blow across the knuckles with a nut-pick. Conversation between my luncheon partner, a desiccated British gentlewoman in flowered chiffon, and myself was somewhat on the desultory side; she seemed astonished that I was not wearing my tomahawk and declared that she had no desire to visit New York as a friend of hers had been gored by a charging bison in Wall Street. Putting her at ease with a few jocose references to the Boston Tea Party, the War of 1812, and one or two similar highlights in Anglo-American relations, I transferred my attention to the Regent on my left. I found him a keen observer of our domestic scene, notably that portion of it centering about Hollywood.

"Based upon your personal experience," he asked with a thoughtful frown, "would you say that Greer Garson wears falsies?" I assured him that my knowledge of the queenly redhead was purely limited to abhorring her from afar, and, to assuage his disappointment, quoted the opinions of eminent workers in the field like Earl Wilson, Sidney Skolsky, et al. From this we progressed to a consideration of the comparative merits of Ann Sheridan, Esther Williams, Mae West, and, inescapably, Jane Russell. I suggested that His Highness toy with the possibility of buying up the latter and moving her piecemeal to Malaya as a curiosity, much in the way William Randolph Hearst used to with Scotch castles, but I gathered he was appalled by the magnitude of the undertaking.

"Well," he said at length, casting a quick glance about the table to make sure everyone was thoroughly tapioca-happy, "now for the *pièce de résistance*—my zoo." We followed with alacrity, remembering wondrous tales told in the bars of Singapore of his prowess as a big-game hunter. And indeed one would have to go a long way to equal the specimens we saw that day in his compound—all the way to a New Jersey chicken farm, in fact. With the exception of three disgruntled parrots who must have slipped in by mistake, the palace zoo consisted of two hundred of the most beat-out fowls conceivable —Plymouth Rocks, White Wyandottes, and Rhode Island Reds. Their master surveyed them tenderly, yet along with his pride I thought I detected a hint of fear in his face. I was right. Suddenly before my eyes all the pomp and circumstance of the monarch fell away and the Tungku Makhota became just a little harassed citizen caught in the economic deadfall. "You know," he said helplessly, in almost the words my father had used twenty-five years before when our poultry farm went down the drain, "those God-damn things'll eat me out of house and home."

There are other vignettes of Johore sharply etched on the memory—our afternoon with the elderly sister of the Sultan, the Tengku Ampuan, a woman of surpassing grace and distinction; the colorful tattoo put on by the Welsh Fusiliers, quite patently to remind the natives that the British lion still had claws; the reckless profusion of orchids on everyone's dinner table, worth hundreds of dollars by New York midwinter standards; and most unforgettable of all, our visit to a rubber estate. There ought to be some kind of insurance policy available whereby the traveler could protect himself against visiting a rubber estate. Unless your name is Harvey Firestone, it is doubtful whether the sight of twelve thousand acres of future hot-water bottles will affect you as the Grecian urn did Keats. For five agonizing hours, under the aegis of a methodical Dane who knew all there was to know about rubber, we were dragged over the largest plantation in Johore and shown it tree by tree. Perhaps I am deficient in what the advertising priesthood refers to as the poetry of big business, but as I stood under a corrugated iron shed, coughing back ammonia fumes and watching the liquid latex dribble out of the centrifuges, it seemed an awful lot of trouble to go to for a simple two-way stretch. But then, knock wood, I don't suffer from middle-aged spread.

Beguiling as was Malaya, it was long since time for us to wend our

way toward Siam, our next destination. Hirschfeld, less impatient than myself, preferred to make the journey by ship, so, presenting him with a pair of Ayvad's water-wings and my blessing, I took off one sweltering morning for Bangkok in a BOAC flying boat. The five-hour trip was comfortable and uneventful, and as we skimmed effortlessly over the hundreds of tiny islands studding the azure waters of the Gulf of Siam, they seemed to sparkle like hundreds of tiny islands studding the Gulf of Siam. Five other passengers shared the cabin—three extremely wretched-looking Chinese, whose eye-balls capsized every time we hit an air pocket, a studious Indian gentleman in massive horn-rimmed spectacles traveling for the Y.M.C.A., and the corpulent, florid-faced representative of an American machinery firm. The latter treated me to the usual diatribe about the alarming inroads of Communism among his servants, the imminent collapse of the democratic ideal due to the fulminations of Henry Wallace, *und so weiter.* When he had concluded and lay back steaming with indignation, the Indian gentleman took over. Producing a stack of back issues of *Reader's Digest,* he read aloud to me in a nasal singsong five or eight dozen of those exhilarating fillers its pages are speckled with—The Cutest Thing My Dog Ever Said, Is Heart-Disease Killing One in Three?, Palo Alto Solves its Sewage Problem, and You Are Never Too Old to Take Up Fencing. He was just graduating into excerpts from Liebman's *Peace of Mind* and Fink's *Release from Nervous Tension,* both of which my system could have used to advantage, when the aircraft providentially glided down to its anchorage in the Klong Toi outside the Siamese capital.

In my innocence I had supposed that hotel accommodations in a city as remote as Bangkok could be had for the asking, but the one European hostelry I managed to discover, the Ratanakosindr, was full up and no amount of cajolery, bribery, or sign language could induce the staff to part with a shakedown. At last, a kindly American film exhibitor saw me seated on a mound of satchels softly sobbing to myself. He blew my nose, stirred up a jeep, and drove me to the home of our military attaché, who, by some telepathy I still cannot fathom, was expecting me. Colonel Randolph, a lanky, affable Texan, had flown with distinction in the Pacific and European theaters, a service for which his country had rather ambiguously rewarded him by thrusting him into the thick of Siamese political intrigue. He put his extensive, airy house and his twelve servants at my disposal, gave me a fatherly talk about the rate of exchange, and, with consummate tact, left me to my own devices.

From the very beginning I was charmed by Bangkok, and I propose to be aggressively syrupy about it in the most buckeye travelogue manner. I liked its polite, gentle, handsome people, its temples, flowers, and canals, the relaxed and peaceful rhythm of life there. Apart from its shrill and tumultuous central thoroughfare swarming with Chinese and Indian bazaars, it struck me as the most soothing metropolis I had thus far seen in the East. Its character is complex and inconsistent; it seems at once to combine the Hannibal, Missouri, of Mark Twain's boyhood with Beverly Hills, the Low Countries, and Chinatown. You pass from populous, glaring streets laden with traffic into quiet country lanes paralleled by canals out of a Dutch painting; a tree-shaded avenue of pretentious mansions set in wide lawns abruptly becomes a bustling row of shops and stalls, then melts into a sunny village of thatched huts among which water buffalo graze. The effect is indescribably pleasing; your eye constantly discovers new vistas, isolated little communities around every corner tempting you to explore them.

Unfortunately it is hot; it was most damnably hot in April, the very peak of Siamese summer, and sightseeing at ninety-six degrees requires stamina. Most of mine evaporated after trudging through the National Museum and a couple of the Siamese wats, or temples, but it was nevertheless a completely rewarding experience. The Temple of the Emerald Buddha, in the monastery adjoining the palace, is mandatory sightseeing. Its flaunting, sportive improvisations of gilt and lacquer, the glass-and-tile mosaics, the bronze Garudas, and the rows of colossal, multi-colored divinities guarding its approaches dazzle an Occidental accustomed to the severity of Greek and Roman architecture. Surrounding the temple, under an arcade extending for blocks, is an extraordinary mural of the Ramayana; one may be forgiven for gushing shamelessly over the taste and technical skill of the artists who wrought it. The National Museum (ignored in all the guidebooks I encountered) contains a superb collection of Buddhas from every part of Southeast Asia, as well as remarkable exhibits of costumes, musical instruments, theater puppets, and artifacts. One of the more touching items is a full-size wheelbarrow and spade of ivory, mother-of-pearl, and ebony made for some vanished princeling; also on view, in a murky corner, is a quaint model engine and tender, the "Victoria," presented by the eminent Queen to King Mongkut, the sovereign of *Anna and the King of Siam.*

With the arrival of Hirschfeld, wan and greenish after five days of smörgåsbord on a Scandinavian tramp (he had not taken a steamer after all but had ridden up on the shoulders of a Scandinavian tramp), my activities became somewhat less cerebral. We squandered a good three dollars on the midget horse-races at the Royal Bangkok Sports Club, flirted outrageously with the cabaret girls at the Cathay, and wandered about the Chinese jewelers' shops in the Ban Moh. Aided by Hirschfeld's expert knowledge of gems and my own shrewd bargaining sense, I was enabled to pick up— at a fraction more than twice what I would have paid for them in America—three emeralds. I had them appraised later in Bombay and was told that they had been cut down from a very rare Coca-Cola bottle. Of course, I had known this at the time I bought them, but preferred not to damage Hirschfeld's self-esteem by mentioning it. Three or four hundred dollars is a small enough price to preserve a friendship, and in any case, I had paid for them in express checks filched from my friend's pants while he lay asleep.

I had but one fault to find with Hirschfeld during these halcyon days: a strange and stubborn fixation, amounting at times to a psychosis, that I might burden our expedition with a little pet or two. It happened that John Royola, who collects wild animals for the Rockefeller Foundation and many American zoological parks, was in Bangkok at the time, preparing to embark a shipment of specimens gathered in Burma, French Indo-China, and Siam. His depot in Bankopi was a fascinating storehouse of elephants, monkeys, and snakes, and we frequently used to drop in to watch him milk the cobras and Russell's vipers, whose crystallized venom is of considerable medical value. One morning I spotted a five-months-old baby elephant, less than a yard high and as cunning as the proverbial bug's ear, wandering around the grounds uprooting the bushes. He seemed to be about the right size for my apartment in New York; I figured I could tether him in the bathroom, and, when he became more robust, the children could ride him to school and economize on bus fares. As Royola, waving my check to dry it, vanished into the house to procure a blue satin bow to tie around the creature's neck, Hirschfeld blew his top.

"I'm through!" he spluttered, his face purple. "I refuse to travel in the same stateroom with that—that pachyderm!"

"Just a second there, Percy," I interrupted, biting the words out between my teeth, "you're talking about a member of my family. I don't interfere in your private life and I'll thank you to keep out of mine." The man's ferocity was startling to behold; he flung himself down in a temper, beat his fists on the earth, and foamed at the chops. It was so alarming, in sooth, that I had to call off the deal to forestall a most certain case of apoplexy. I could see Royola thought my crony's conduct extravagant; he offered to sell me something more compact, like a half-grown leopard or a banded krait, but Hirschfeld was inflexible. No doubt his years of urban living had atrophied that love of animals, that kinship toward things that creep and crawl, which Mother Nature endows us with at birth.

It is one of the profound limitations of the human spirit that even when we are at our most content, some obscure demon goads us on our way. We might have remained forever at Colonel Randolph's, gobbling his food, swilling his whiskey, and tyrannizing his servants; indeed, so amiable was he I think we might almost have forced him out of his house altogether; but in less than a month the itch for new horizons was on us. There came a morning, inevitably, when we stood again at the airport, wringing his hand in farewell, bound back to Singapore and the steamer that would take us on to India.

"Goodbye, goodbye!" he called as the powerful motors rose in volume, "I'll never forget you, boys!" And well might he say so, for in our luggage, unbeknownst to him, reposed his best spoons, his wife's diamond clips, and three of his dress shirts. There he stood, erect and soldierly, a symbol of all that was best and most generous in the American way of life. Was it any wonder a lump formed in our throats as we waved adieu to Siam? Was it any wonder a second lump formed on top of the first one at the prospect of paying room rent and board again? Was it any wonder? Now I ask you.

7

The Back of Beyond

I F YOU had chanced to stray into the Western & Occidental Hotel in Penang, Malaya, during the ensuing fortnight (and if you did, you ought to have your head examined), you might have observed a curious derelict brooding over a lemon squash in the lobby. The four-day growth of beard, the feverish deep-sunk eyes, the nicotine-stained fingers, and the grimy singlet all told their pitiful but familiar tale of the beachcomber, yet another white man doomed to disintegration under the remorseless tropical sun. Could this brutish mass of protoplasm, one asked himself, really be a thinking, sentient human organism? Could this seedy castaway, mottled with heat rash and bereft of illusions, be the same buoyant pilgrim who had left New York just five months before, his head stuffed with romantic visions and his satchels with nylon hose? Could this bit of flotsam cast up on a lee shore, spurned by civilization and totally dormant above the neckband, conceivably be the author of these present lines? Brother, I hope to kiss a pig he could.

What made my imbroglio especially grievous, of course, was the fact that I had nobody to blame for it but myself. I had flown down from Siam to Singapore with Hirschfeld, only to discover that the *President Monroe*, which was to convey us to India, was lallygagging around somewhere in the South China Sea and would not arrive for at least twelve days. After two memorable nights at the Raffles Hotel, where we shared a mildewed lazarette with three other dupes and choked down what impressed me as the most odious cuisine in Asia, I threw in the towel. Why crucify ourselves in the heat and tedium of Singapore, I argued, when colorful Penang, with its superb beaches, horticultural gardens, and luxury hotels lay a day's journey distant up the peninsula? Since the ship was calling there anyway, the trip would be pure lagniappe, an extra dash of stardust unforeseen in our program. My logic was unassailable and my presentation masterly; but whether through inertia or some mysterious instinct that protects the feeble-minded, Hirschfeld refused to budge. Assuring him he was missing the experience of a lifetime, I engaged a compartment on the Malayan Railway, bid adieu to the Raffles in a philippic that shriveled the manager to a heap of volcanic ash, and squared away.

The first part of the journey, though boring, was supportable; the train wheezed along through endless miles of rubber estates, swampy jungle, and rather squalid villages, pausing at intervals to take on cordwood for the locomotive and permit buffalo gnats to batten on my blood. At Kuala Lumpur, the government seat, a dandy

A curious derelict brooding over lemon squash

little surprise awaited me—all the first-class sleeping carriages were full up. I threatened, pleaded, ranted to no avail. Eventually I was bedded down in the second-class car, a weird affair of fourteen open bunks set in double tiers, stifling hot and crammed with Chinese, Malays, and Tamils. Every fifteen minutes during the night, a drenching tropical downpour swept in through the open windows, sluicing us out of our berths. About four o'clock, as we were daw-dling in a station, someone outside flung in a banana peel which settled on my chest. My visit to the Pasteur Institute in Bangkok had made me a wee bit snake-conscious, and when I felt the clammy embrace, I naturally assumed a fer-de-lance was pitching woo at me. Fortunately, I had enough presence of mind to open my mouth and discharge a piercing scream. The signal penetrated to the caboose, and hastening forward, the conductor extricated me from the wash-room where I had barricaded myself. In a few moments, under his calming influence, hysteria was restored, and with many a light-hearted chuckle we proceeded on our way.

All together I spent three and a half weeks in Penang before the *President Monroe* nosed over the horizon, and this much I will say for it: if you ever want a perfect honeymoon spot, a place where scenery and climate fuse to produce unadulterated witchery, where life has the tremulous sweetness of a plucked lute-string and dark-ness falls all too soon, go to the Hotel Plaza in New York. Of all the lethargic, benighted, somnolent flea-bags this side of Hollywood, the port of Georgetown on the island of Penang is the most abysmal. At the time I was there, its recreational facilities consisted of four Tar-zan films, a dance hall housing eighty-five pock-marked Malay de-linquents, a funicular railway, and a third-rate beach situated five miles from nowhere. If, after exhausting the potentialities of these, you retained any appetite for sightseeing, you could visit the Ayer Itam temple and the botanical gardens. The former is possibly the largest, and unquestionably the dullest, Buddhist temple in Malaya, and no wastebasket is complete without a snapshot of this historic shrine. The botanical gardens boast many varieties of cactus not found anywhere, not even in the botanical gardens. The day I was there, I waited almost three minutes for them to show up, but

85

never caught so much as a glimpse of anything resembling a cactus. I related the incident subsequently to a group of passengers aboard ship who were discussing occasions on which they had failed to find cacti, and it was unanimously agreed that my experience was by far the most unusual.

I doubt if anyone short of Dante could describe the cookery at the Western & Occidental Hotel; I have heard it defended on the ground that it is no worse than the fare in any British colonial hotel, which is like saying that measles is no worse than virus pneumonia. The meal usually led off with an eerie gumbo identified as pumpkin soup, puce in color and dysenteric in effect. This was followed by a crisp morsel of the fish called *selango*r for want of a more scathing term, reminiscent in texture of a Daniel Green comfy slipper fried in deep fat. The roast was a pale, resilient scintilla of mutton that turned the tines of the fork, garnished with a spoonful of greenish boiled string and a dab of penicillin posing as a potato. For dessert there was *gula Malacca*, a glutinous blob of sago swimming in skimmed milk and caramel syrup, so indescribably saccharine that it produced a singing in the ears and screams of anguish from the bridge-work. As the diner stiffened slowly in his chair, his features settling into the ghastly smile known as the *risus sardonicus*, the waiter administered the *coup de grâce*, a savory contrived of a moldy sardine spread-eagled on a bit of blackened toast. The exact nature of the thimbleful of rusty brown fluid that concluded the repast was uncertain. The only other time I saw it, awash in the scuppers of the *President Monroe*, the sailors called it bilge.

Between the food, the night life, and the uncompromisingly stiff-necked British vacationists guffawing over their pahits and sundowners, it was not very long before I was gibbering with loneliness. My two or three attempts to scrape acquaintance were greeted with the welcome commonly accorded a typhoid carrier. At length, by assiduously cultivating the Chinese night clerk and consenting to smuggle him into the States so that he could marry Barbara Stanwyck, I cadged an invitation to accompany him to his swimming club. We bathed in a tepid, oily swell dotted with fruit rinds and then adjourned to the clubhouse, where we sat in exquisite discomfort on broken rattan chairs, sipping orange crush and masochistically allowing chickens to peck at our bare tootsies. My companion's conversation, though voluble, was somewhat ambiguous; I listened brightly for a full hour to a panegyric on Dale Carnegie under the impression that he referred to the late-lamented Scotch philanthropist. The afternoon, nevertheless, was not wholly unproductive. Within forty-eight hours, I developed a dramatic fungus growth in the left ear indistinguishable from the mushroom the botanists call the Destroying Angel and ascribed by the doctor to bathing in contaminated water. Thanks to sulfanilamide, I was at least spared the final indignity of hobbling into old age brandishing an ear trumpet, but when kind hands assisted me up the Jacob's ladder of the *Monroe*, I was Lazarus risen from the dead.

Over the first decent coffee I had drunk in months, I poured out my doleful tale to Hirschfeld, but his malemute code contained no such word as compassion. Immediately upon my departure, he had fallen in with the wastrel set in Singapore and thereafter had lived like a debutante, guzzling Bollinger '23 and fresh Beluga caviar and roistering till the cows came home; indeed, on one occasion the cows were home three hours, milked, scrubbed, and chewing their cud in their stalls and Hirschfeld was still roistering. If I had any consolation, it was in the thought that Penang was now merely a memory. The moment I evolved that profound bit of philosophy, Fate drew back and gave me another boot in the derrière. For five livelong days, the *Monroe* lay alongside the wharf in the unspeakable heat while a gang of rachitic coolies listlessly transferred seventeen hundred tons of tin and rubber into her hold. As if our cup were not already full to overflowing, a fresh affliction arose; swarms of tiny man-eating midges from the freighter next to us invaded our cabins, brocading our milk-white skins with revolting scarlet weals. When the shoreline of Penang finally receded into the haze, I knelt down on the deck and spontaneously yielded up thanks for my deliverance. I arose with twin splotches of tar disfiguring my only pair of slacks, but I was in no mood to split hairs.

We made the run across the Indian Ocean to Ceylon in four days; it was the season of the southwest monsoon, marked by leaden, overcast skies and frequent squalls. Most of the ship's ninety-odd passengers were branch managers and representatives of American firms like International Harvester, Standard Oil, and Goodyear Rubber, bound home on leave or en route to other stations. They were a glum, abstracted lot who laughed little and spent the day discussing freight rates and tariffs. The only thing distinguishing us from the Sedalia Chamber of Commerce was the small contingent of Spaniards, Italians, and specious Central Europeans with cropped bullet heads and saber-cuts on their cheeks. The latter fervidly assured you that they were Swiss, but they showed a suspicious tendency to prick up their ears and whinny whenever a Strauss waltz was played. Far and away the most spectacular character on the ship, and a little whiff of gelignite that at times bid fair to explode the whole male passenger complement, was Mrs. Fuscher.

Mr. Fuscher, a tall, mealy German said to have been a very eminent Nazi in the employ of I. G. Farbenindustrie in Shanghai, was espoused to a lady who, to put it mildly, had been richly endowed. Every time she strode on deck in the pitifully brief halter and shorts she affected, eyes popped like champagne corks and strong men sobbed aloud. It did not seem possible that mere wisps of silk could confine such voluptuous charms; in fact, there were those who lived in the hope that a truant gust of wind might create a sensational diversion. On one occasion, I lashed myself to the brink of nervous collapse reading the same sentence over and over in Motley's *Rise of the Dutch Republic*, desperately trying to ignore Mrs. Fuscher as she stood silhouetted against the sun in a diaphanous sports dress. I thought it rather poor sportsmanship of Hirschfeld, incidentally, to show her a sketch of his representing me as a wolf baying against the moon, when he himself was so patently on the prowl.

Fuscher, needless to say, was fully aware of the electricity his wife generated and took care to guard her like the Jonker diamond. Then, by a stroke of luck, he was suddenly taken seasick, and it was every man for himself. I saw my chance during boat drill when I encountered the lovely creature hopelessly ensnared in her life-jacket, fluttering like a wounded bird. I quickly drew her into a dark companionway and managed to squeeze her into it properly, though it naturally required a certain amount of fussing with the straps. Just as she was giggling, "What are you doing, you foolish boy?," Hirschfeld slithered around the corner in his typically sneaky fashion.

"Hey, that's no way to put on a lifejacket," he snapped, shouldering me aside. "The tapes go over the front, like this." I let him demonstrate his method for what it was worth (and it was worth plenty, judging from the hammerlock he took on Mrs. Fuscher). We had almost reached the tickling stage when I glanced up accidentally and beheld Mr. Fuscher, arms akimbo, glowering down at us.

"What is the meaning of this—this *Schweinerei?*" he grunted. His wife blubbered out a breathless account of how helpful the American cavaliers had been, but he cut it short midway and marched her off. It was just as well, for the man was patently a dangerous lunatic of some sort and might easily have misconstrued our kindness to his wife. Traveling about the world in these disturbed times, one cannot be too careful to avoid situations like the foregoing, where perfectly laudable motives may lead to the gravest consequences.

As the days wore on, one other personality on board came into bold relief, that of Armand Brissac, the quartermaster. Monsieur Brissac was a grizzled, dapper individual of indeterminate age who confided to the unwary that he had circumnavigated the earth thirty-seven times, exclusive of having made myriad side trips into outlying parishes like the Gran Chaco, Nyassaland, the Gobi Desert, Baffin Bay, and Easter Island. The results of all this gypsying, he added, were codified in nineteen massive scrapbooks he planned to bequeath to the Smithsonian, and if the two I examined were any criterion, the collection may one day emerge as the largest gallery of pin-up girls in the world. Outside of a few faded postcards of the Canal Zone and Starlight Park, the albums contained nothing but thousands of snapshots of simpering young ladies in various stages of deshabille—all taken at his beach house in Venice, California, he solemnly assured me, in a spirit of the strictest scientific inquiry. It was obvious to anyone that Brissac's hobby had cost him an immense outlay of energy and money, and he made no secret of the fact that his lifework was far from complete. "These are just Ameri-

*Eyes popped like champagne corks
and strong men sobbed aloud*

can types," he explained offhandedly. "Before I'm finished, the record will embrace babes from every race on earth." The precise anthropological value of Brissac's library of cheesecake was, I must admit, a trifle dubious, but even if posterity denies him a place in the pantheon of science, his name will rank for single-mindedness of purpose with those of Casanova and Daddy Browning.

A general strike was in process at the city of Colombo when we reached it, and our anticipated two-day stay there was shortened to a matter of twelve hours. It was a keen disappointment, alleviated in part by a pleasant and quite unexpected compliment I received from the passport control officer. Following the usual inspection of visas and landing permits, he came up to me rather hesitantly.

"Do you mind if I tell you something?" he asked with a shy smile. "I've been stamping passports for years, but I'd just like to say that yours is one of the prettiest I've ever seen. It's done with real taste —not like *some* I could mention. May I ask who did it?" I revealed that I had most of my things done by a little old man in a side street who could copy anything and whose prices, consequently, were cheaper because he was out of the high rent district. "I knew it!" he said triumphantly. "That chap's an artist—he's going places." I told him about several places the old man had already been, and we parted with a warm exchange of handclasps, one of which I later brought back to my wife as a gift.

There is a widespread popular belief, no doubt fostered by obsolete geography books, that Ceylon's fame derives from her production of much of the world's tea crop. The notion is a completely erroneous one. The principal industry of the island is the manufacture of souvenir ebony elephants, cunningly constructed in such a way that the tusks and ears break off the moment one's ship is out of sight of land. This leaves the tourist with a misshapen chunk of wood that can be used effectively as either paperweight or missile, depending on his ability to adjust himself to local conditions. Luckily, Hirschfeld and I had been warned that unscrupulous curio dealers might try to palm off indestructible elephants on us and were very much on our guard. After trudging ceaselessly from shop

Family Group, Ceylon

to shop and deliberating over thousands of carvings, we managed
to stumble on a truly gruesome pair which fulfilled every qualifica-
tion and fell apart before we even reached the gangplank. We also
acquired an impressive harvest of tortoise-shell combs, brass slop-
jars suitable for transplanting ferns, bamboo fans imported from
South Attleboro, Massachusetts, and a pair of ingenious fly-whisks
made of aigrettes and carabao horn. Apparently someone from the
ship must have pointed us out as tourists (certainly nobody could
have deduced it from seeing us stroll up the street toting our gim-
cracks), for a citizen with a knapsack and flute materialized shortly
and conned us into angeling a fight between a mongoose and a
cobra. For sheer, unalloyed excitement, the spectacle was easily as
thrilling as any ballet Martha Graham ever devised; the varmints,
so heavily doped that you could smell the barbital a block away,
persistently got into a clinch worthy of Ingrid Bergman and Cary
Grant and slobbered each other with kisses. The serpent finally vanished down a sewer, and disgorging a sizable slug of valuta to cover
the loss, we slunk off to the vessel, bitterly denouncing ourselves for
our imbecility.

Two days later, the *Monroe* slowly edged her way into the Alex-
andra Docks at Bombay and we stood on the threshold of India
at last, salt-caked and battered by tempests but dauntless, our pil-
lowcases bursting with soiled laundry, our pocketbooks tenanted
only by bats, but hungry withal for the enchantments that lay ahead.
To the politicians and religious leaders, the industrialists, lawyers,
doctors, and members of the press who crowded about us piteously
pleading for the one word that might resolve the difficulties be-
setting their land, our answer was always the same, "Not yet, fellows—see us at the end of the week." We might have put them off
with some all-too-facile phrase, but custodians of the American
Way that we were, true uptown Yankee Doodle boys, we knew the
obligation that lay heavy on us: to walk softly and carry a big suitcase. It was a pretty important assignment a couple of middle-aged
kids had chosen, to straighten out India's four hundred teeming mil-
lions by the time the *President Polk* came through a fortnight later,
but we had two things on our side—plain old-fashioned gumption

and lots of American know-how. We didn't know where we were going or how we'd get there, but we knew one thing—when we got there, we'd be there. And that's something, even if it's nothing.

The serpent finally vanished down a sewer

8

It's Not the Heat

It's the Cupidity

THE CUBICLE was tiny, dark, and breathlessly hot, but the lackluster Indian official who occupied it and who was engaged in passing a couple of American camels through the needle's eye of the Bombay police was even tinier, darker, and hotter. Spread out on the rickety table before him, the welter of affidavits, permits, cards of identity, and mimeographed applications kept sifting to the floor like snowflakes as he scratched away painstakingly, recording in quadruplicate such momentous information as the birthplace of our great-grandparents, our Social Security numbers, the precise quantity of freckles on our buttocks. The morning sun rose higher in the heavens and the room became suffocating. Bathed in perspiration, panting like draft animals, Hirschfeld and I numbly watched our dossiers being woven into the vast crazy quilt of the Alien Registration Section. From time to time, as if to reassure himself that our photographs had not undergone some subtle transformation like the portrait of Dorian Gray, the clerk would whip open our passports and narrowly scan our faces.

"You are S. J. Hirschfeld, you say?"

"Well, that's my name, but not my initials. They're his."

"But his name is Albert Perelman. I have it written down here."

"It's a mistake. The initials belong to the opposite names." The official's face brightened; he knew there was something shady about us.

"Ah, so," he said hopefully. "Then the initials are made out wrong."

"No, no—they're the right initials, but the wrong *man*."

"Exactly. The passports are clearly not in order." He rose triumphantly and shoveled up a random armful of papers. "Follow me." By sheer noise, gesticulation, and, inevitably, a folded ten-rupee note circumspectly shoved under the blotter, we browbeat the man into perceiving his error. Grumbling sourly, he resumed his minute scrutiny of our credentials. Weeks, years, epochs passed; dynasties rose and fell, and still the idiot bureaucrat chewed his penholder and deliberated whether our presence in India ran counter to regulation. The other visas, though they were completely outside his jurisdiction, fascinated him unbearably; he continually held them up to the light, grumbled over the stamps, and clucked appreciation of their terminology. At length, his last flimsy pretext gone, he affixed his chop with infinite bad grace and the maximum amount of fussing with rubber stamps. Three hours after the portals of the Criminal Investigation Division had swallowed us up, we reeled into the street with the grudging permission of the authorities freely to pass—provided, of course, that we signified our intention to leave, reported to the police promptly on arrival, and informed the Bombay Residency immediately of our return. We were in India, the newest jewel in the diadem of freedom.

Like the half-dozen other passengers debarking from the *President Monroe*, Hirschfeld and I had made a beeline at once for the Taj Hotel, a huge Mauro-Gothic edifice of gray stone whose crenelated towers, battlements, and drawbridges more accurately suggested a college dormitory. Much of Bombay's Victorian architecture, in fact, was singularly reminiscent of the campus of a third-rate Ohio university; more than once I could have sworn I heard the ghostly plunk of banjos and the faint despairing bleat of freshmen being paddled. Whatever European and Indian social life had emerged since the war was centered about the Taj, but it was still a rather sickly plant. The tense political feeling between Hindu and Moslem, the riots at Amritsar, Lahore, Calcutta, and the North-West Frontier, and widespread public apprehension about India's future after the British withdrawal dampened the few visible attempts at gaiety. To add to the universal gloom, all alcoholic beverages had been banned in the area two days a week, with the promise that before long the city would be completely dry. Neither of us was particularly intuitive, but we had not been exposed to the sweltering heat and dullness of Bombay very long before we realized that we had bought a pig in a poke.

Our hotel room did nothing to help matters. It was a long, monastic cell facing a courtyard, extremely hot, and so narrow that two persons could not pass without scarifying each other's skins. Someone had made a halfhearted gesture in the direction of cooling it by installing an overhead fan capable of two full revolutions a minute; most of the time it served as a trysting-place for flies. The bathroom was a masterpiece of irony. Without either window or toilet—two European fripperies scorned by the management—it was equipped with a set of double doors which, if closed, sealed you in hermetically until you fainted; if left open, exposed your questionable charms to the approval of the entire courtyard. In this unwholesome burrow, flanked by eleven pieces of luggage and grilled by temperatures that hovered in the upper nineties, we dwelt through the first week of our sojourn in India. It might be supposed that the effect of such propinquity in record heat would be to lacerate our tempers, to make us impatient of one another's shortcomings. Far from it; never once did Hirschfeld try to brain me with the commode or I to sever his jugular vein, dearly as we would have loved to. If a point of difference rose between us, we settled it calmly, like gentlemen; we merely fell shrieking on the bed, beat the bolster with doubled fists until our tantrums subsided, and then sulked for two days. I think it will always stand as a tribute to my geniality and unruffled calm that Hirschfeld was finally able to issue from that room under his own power rather than on an undertaker's trestle. In the hands of anyone less tranquil, he might today be wearing a dainty aluminum cloche on his noggin.

In the unending steamy heat, when the smallest physical gesture sent a cascade of sweat coursing down the spine, the days took on the remote, insubstantial quality of a dream. In the mornings we dutifully went sightseeing, toiling up Malabar Hill to the Parsee towers of silence or out to the Elephanta Caves; in the afternoons,

Noonday mirage, Old Delhi

having clubbed ourselves with an inferior curry washed down with countless chota pegs, we drifted spiritlessly through the shops in Hornby Road, acquiring those curious knickknacks—the bangles, the brocades, and the Buddhas—which arouse such cries of admiration from the family circle and are forthwith relegated to the attic. We began to sort out familiar faces at the hotel—import-exporters we had run into at Shanghai, Singapore, and Bangkok, strange faceless men who moved energetically between the great Eastern cities manipulating mysterious deals and glibly discussing the complexities of foreign exchange. They are a baffling tribe, these import-exporters. They are dapper, knowledgeable, worldly, and altogether elusive. I met scores of them, became convivial on their expense accounts, shared quarters with them, and cooed over snapshots of their babies; but no amount of devious, cunning questioning could elicit just what they were importing or exporting. Once in a while, one would drop a seemingly careless hint that twelve thousand gross of needles or saccharine laid down in Teheran or Jogjakarta would double a man's money, yet if you asked him point-blank if he was in the needle or saccharine business, he would give you a crafty, inscrutable wink and change the subject. It struck me as an ideal occupation—you traveled in romantic lands, lived in luxury hotels, answered no man's bidding, incurred none of the hazards of the secret agent. Had I been able to crash my way into their confidence, I would have cheerfully forsworn belles-lettres without a backward glance.

The morning came when, by a superhuman effort of the will, we shook off our torpor and struck out for New Delhi, determined to see at least a portion of the country before we gave it back to the Indians. Flying north at nine thousand feet, it was possible to breathe again and pity Hirschfeld, who, with a lively concern for Hirschfeld, was creeping along the burning, barren waste in a railway carriage. At Ahmedabad, where we stopped to refuel, the airdrome restaurant showed splendid contempt for the 102-degree heat by serving cornflakes and scalding hot milk; the stewards presented it with an elaborate flourish, plainly bent on demonstrating that the airline was run with Amerikanski tempo. I came up the ramp at New Delhi with the inexplicable sensation of having seen it all before—the intolerably bright, dry heat, the artificial sky, the trim airport buildings. Then I remembered why. Except for the turbaned porters eying me with hangdog avarice, it might have been Barstow, Phoenix, any one of a dozen Western desert towns. My heart, avid for romance, leaped up at the stately row of camels near the newsstand, but when I drew nigh I saw they were only an advertisement for some obscure Yankee cigarette.

Driving through the tremendous hexagonal parks and plazas that crisscross New Delhi, one has to admit that New Delhi is certainly crisscrossed with tremendous hexagonal parks and plazas. The perspectives are overpowering—endless tree-lined boulevards sweeping up to gigantic official buildings, grandiose monuments that dominate mile-long vistas, everywhere a sense of organized planning that offers a sardonic contrast to the confusion of the politicians behind the façade. The same disparity was obvious at the Imperial, the spacious, ultra-modern hotel where my taxi deposited me. Though I was the only prospective guest in sight, the three Indian clerks instantly gave way to mass hysteria. No, my telegram requesting a reservation had not arrived; the house was full to overflowing, people were sleeping in the corridors; they were expecting a congress of rajahs and could not possibly book a room for at least five months. Eventually the clamor subsided—it was manifestly the normal routine—and I was assigned a suite already tenanted by a corpulent young British officer in the Royal Engineers. Major Fishguard was seated in the living room in his birthday suit, sipping whiskey and water and studying a flyblown copy of *Screen Secrets*. He insisted on pouring a small libation on the altar of friendship, which I accepted, of course, on purely medicinal grounds. He then proceeded to expound the highly original philosophy that a bird cannot fly with only one wing and followed it up with a number of dividends. For an Englishman, the major was fairly garrulous; I learned he had been in the Indian Army twenty of his thirty-seven years, was stationed at Rawalpindi in the Punjab, and felt that, all things considered, Betty Grable was the girl he would most like to shack up with. We were still discussing variations on this latter theme five hours afterward when Hirschfeld straggled in, spent and cavernous-eyed from his journey. Any thought of dinner, naturally, was sacrilegious until he could catch up with us, and though he tried manfully, he went down with colors flying. The last thing I recall that evening was the major and myself, heads swathed in improvised turbans made of towels, solemnly beating time on empty bottles with a swagger stick and harmonizing "Pale Hands I Love."

By a happy circumstance, I had encountered in Bombay the American air attaché from New Delhi, who had amiably offered us his quarters for our stay, and we lost no time taking possession next morning. It was a gift verging on the princely, for along with the five-room apartment went a head bearer, two room bearers, a sweeper, a chauffeur, and a sedan, not to mention the privilege of eating in the American mess. One look at the tempting shops in Connaught Circle told us that if we were ever going to see any landmarks, we had better get it over with quickly, so out came the guidebooks and off we went. Our eyes bulged appropriately at the 234-foot Kutub Minar, the tallest single tower in the world and an eminence favored by suicides; a beautiful lovelorn maharanee is reported to have cast herself from it several years ago, but she was probably the same old Indian chieftain's daughter whose legend sanctifies so many Lover's Leaps in our own country. At the burning ghats, where the Hindus cremate their dead, we stood about morbidly staring at three or four mounds of ashes that had no real significance; in the fierce glare of midday, on this eroded riverbank, the impact of the dissolution of the flesh was as paltry as a Boy Scout wienie roast. In the Red Fort at Old Delhi, we trudged miles on swollen feet to see the Peacock Throne, a rather ordinary morris chair made of marble around which skulked a crew of pustular beggars ululating for baksheesh. The Chandni Chauk, or Silver Street, of the old town, nevertheless, was all that had been predicted, even if it was 110 in the shade the afternoon we explored it. It was something out of the Arabian Nights—the incredible, fantastic turmoil, the swarming crowds, the gargantuan bullocks asleep in the roadway, the bazaars with their Benares silks and Kashmir woolens, glass and silver jewelry, and Punjabi shoes. You wanted to buy everything in sight, including a few of those sloe-eyed gazelles in saris, and they were prepared to sell it. Only a humane regard for our chauffeur, who was quietly melting away in the sun like a dish of butter, finally recalled us to our senses.

The ivory shops in Connaught Circle, though, proved to be our real financial Waterloo. By the time the chaffering died down, we had bought enough gold-embroidered evening bags, antique necklaces, powder jars, paper cutters, cocktail forks, Mogul miniatures, and book-ends to supply the population of a small Midwestern city (Fort Wayne). The proprietors of the Ivory Palace and the Ivory Mart are unquestionably the world's most consummate salesmen. You are lured into the rear of the shop with nods and becks and wreathed smiles, plied with cooling drinks, and given a thorough coating of Mohammedan schmaltz that lowers your sales resistance to the vanishing point. Then, very casually, there is introduced some exquisite trifle, a four-hundred-year-old bit of Jaipur enamel or a filigreed ivory box—merely as a curiosity, you understand, the shopkeeper beseeches you not to sully his friendship by any thought of purchase. As the victim's blood slowly comes to the boil, more curiosities appear: ivory tusks whose roses or hunting scenes in low relief were three years in the carving, superb bracelets and rings encrusted with gems, chessmen of unbelievable artistry and astronomical cost. I knew that we had definitely broken with reality when I suddenly discovered Hirschfeld haggling for a six-piece bedroom suite of carved ivory, priced at seven hundred thousand rupees, which had taken two men twenty-five years to complete. Why he wanted to possess all this dead tooth structure is beyond me, but he refused to yield to my entreaties and I ultimately had to hit him from behind with a knotted towel and drag him outside before his judgment returned.

We made the 122-mile trip to the Taj Mahal at Agra with a certain amount of trepidation; the famous tomb has inspired so much ecstatic nonsense, so many bad water colors, statuettes, ceramics, paperweights, and postcards, that we were convinced we must be disappointed. Our fears were groundless, for it turned out to be one of the major emotional experiences of the entire journey, despite the

The proprietors of the Ivory Palace and the Ivory Mart are unquestionably the world's most consummate salesmen

insupportable heat, the abysmal food, and the banalities of the
guides. Seen in the first pale flush of sunrise, with a cool wind stir-
ring the treetops in the adjacent gardens, it has the fragile delicacy
of a soap bubble; no other building I have ever seen has conveyed
to me quite that degree of airy grace, of absolute purity. It demands
a strenuous effort on the visitor's part, however, to enjoy it privately.
At every turn he is beset by a horde of cringing, smarmy mendicants chanting facts and figures and whining for alms. Historians

assert that Shah Jehan built the Taj to commemorate his wife Mumtaz Mahal, called the Ornament of the Palace, but if you believe the ceaseless patter of the guides, Lord Curzon, onetime Viceroy of India, deserves the lion's share of the credit. "Lord Curzon's lamp, sahib—presented by Lord Curzon at a cost of five thousand rupees," they jabber. "All these fountains donated by Lord Curzon . . . ninety thousand rupees. . . . Lord Curzon gave these steps out of his own pocket—twelve thousand rupees, sahib . . . this pool gift of noble Lord Curzon . . . rupees . . . Curzon . . . rupees." We backed out through the beautiful red sandstone gate bestowing a pox on the noble lord, grateful nonetheless for at least that first moment of revelation.

Sleep was impossible that night in the hotel at Agra; we sat in the lobby drinking quarts of gin-and-tonic and staring limply at the angry red 104 on the thermometer. The people in the wing opposite ours had dragged their white iron bedsteads out on the lawn and lay gasping in the orbit of an electric fan. By noon the temperature had risen to 115; roaring back to New Delhi, the air that swept in through the car windows was as searing as a blast furnace. There were wild peacocks and baboons under the trees edging the road; villages newly burned out by Moslems and Hindus flicked by every few miles; but every ounce of interest and initiative evaporated under the single fact of the inhuman, punishing sun. In spirit, if not in actuality, we were already aboard the *President Polk;* the vision of her air-conditioned dining room, I am sure, was the only thing that sustained us through that inferno. Ahead of us, if we only knew it, were further ordeals: the ship delayed interminably, weeks of waiting in Bombay, undreamed-of ennui. The Moving Finger had writ, all right, nor all our calamine lotion could wipe out a word of it. Yet somewhere, at the rainbow's end, was an ice-cold shower, a tall glass beaded with moisture, letters from home. *Per aspera ad astra,* ran the motto on my life insurance policy; come prickly heat, come sunstroke, those chaps at Prudential were betting on me to win through. In that sign, God willing, I would conquer.

9

Bile on the Nile

FITFUL GUSTS of rain drove against the windows of the promenade deck; the ship hung suspended for an eternity, quivered as if mortally stricken, and dipped sickeningly forward into the Arabian Sea. The plump Midwestern clubwoman in the deck-chair adjoining mine exhaled a lugubrious groan that culminated in a graveyard knell and plucked weakly at my sleeve. The tortured, queasy face she turned toward me was Lovat green.

"I'm going to die," she whimpered. "I want to die in my stateroom. Help me up."

"Help yourself up, you old bag," I returned chivalrously, closing my eyes to blot out the avalanche of water rearing over us to starboard. Telegraphing my innards to stand at the ready for another plunge into the abyss, I hunched myself into a prenatal ball. Speedier than any toboggan descending the Mount Hovenberg run, the ship plummeted down the hundred-foot slope, rolling over joyously like a sheepdog. Liver and colon, lung and lights, all the shiny interior plumbing I had amassed so painstakingly in dribs and drabs over the years, fused into a single hard knot and wedged in my epiglottis. I had just drawn a long shuddering gasp and girded myself for the next glissando when a familiar hearty voice addressed me.

"What cheer, Netop?" it inquired. "Feeling a bit peckish?" I opened a tentative eye and beheld Hirschfeld bending over me solicitously. His cheeks glowed with rude health and he exuded an aura of limitless animal energy. In his suit of snowy drill, a linen cap rakishly tilted back on his head in the fashion of the great racing

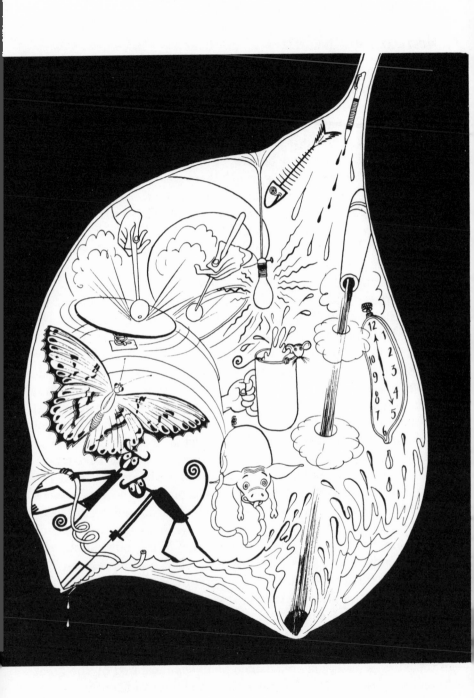

109

driver, Ralph di Palma, he might have stepped straight out of a four-color laxative advertisement. He was vibrant, sprightly, diligent, the epitome of vigorous optimism and dash, and had I had the strength I would have unhesitatingly cut his throat from ear to ear.

"Go away," I croaked miserably. "Go back to the Breakfast Club in Los Angeles where you belong." My voice cracked into a sob. "You cheerleader you." With a heartless snigger, Hirschfeld straightened up, re-lit the noisome cigar stub in his teeth, and skipped off to the sports deck to resume his game of shuffleboard. Wheezing painfully, I lay back in the chair and, as the *President Polk* wallowed on toward Aden buffeted by the southwest monsoon, somberly reviewed the events of the past fortnight.

We had crawled back to Bombay from New Delhi in a state of bleary disrepair, thoroughly dehydrated by the savage midsummer heat but starry-eyed at the prospect of quitting India, when Kismet, working hand in glove with the steamship company, had again put her knee into our groin. Our next carrier, the *President Polk*, already a week overdue, was delayed another four days; flouting the schedule, not to speak of the common laws of decency, she had put into a whistle stop on the Malabar Coast called Cochin to pick up a cargo of cashew nuts. There was no recourse but to move back into the Taj Hotel and somehow bridge the interval until she appeared. The ensuing week was in many respects the most harrowing I have ever lived through. The reader may get some approximate notion of the discomfort we underwent if he dons a cable-stitch sweater, swallows three gallons of hot lemonade, and locks himself in his shoe-closet on an August afternoon. Sicklied o'er with the pale cast of heat lotion, we sat morosely in the lounge, biting our cuticle and drinking endless Collinses that only intensified our depression. The night life of Bombay is roughly on a par with that of Schwenksville, Pennsylvania; if a natural sense of discretion prevents you from visiting the notorious cages, you are thrown back on a half-dozen cinemas exhibiting third-run American movies or slumbrous Hindustani films too recherché for the Western patron. We viewed one of the latter, a historical epic named *Shahjehan* inspired by the great Mogul emperor, for four hours without the faintest idea of what was taking place, other than that it seemed to be full of old silent-picture emblems like roses with falling petals, candles guttering out, and bleeding hearts transfixed by daggers. Two nights later an unidentified hothead flung a grenade into this very theater, expunging eleven taxpayers. The newspapers stated that the outrage was caused by religious bitterness, but obviously some enraged customer, with more gumption than myself, was merely venting his opinion of the feature.

The arrival of the *President Polk*, instead of providing a merciful release from bondage, only brought fresh exasperations. For a full week she lay out in the roads unable to berth, owing to overcrowded docking facilities. Hirschfeld and I prowled the waterside like panthers, eying her yearningly and dreaming of the steaks and blueberry pie just out of reach. In our overwrought imagination, she began to take on an unreal luster; we pictured her bar crowded with dazzling, lonely beauties sipping champagne cocktails, we fancied we heard the unbearable anguish of Louis Armstrong's trumpet echoing across the water, we reached such a degree of self-hypnosis that we could almost smell the pungency of the alcohol flame under the crêpes Suzette. When she finally came alongside, her passengers were stunned to behold two creatures that once were men, half-hysterical and babbling incoherently, blowing kisses to them and behaving for all the world like March hares: so much so, in fact, that a March hare which had come down to the steamer to meet a friend was observed to avert its face contemptuously and extrude its lip in what could only have been a smile of disdain.

Once the first giddy exultation of being aboard had worn off, disillusion came soon enough. For six days during which the temperature hovered in the high nineties, the *President Polk* clove to the dock receiving goatskins and cinnamon. I am seldom capable of sustained rapture; I can thrill to Benny Goodman playing "Stealin' Apples" or a seascape by Marsden Hartley, but I may as well confess freely that goatskins and cinnamon leave me cold. Speaking practically, when you have seen one bale of either, you have seen them all. After the five hundredth, the unending whir and crash of the slings became an abomination. Not the smallest breeze penetrated to the basin where we were tied up; day and night the metal hull of the ship gave off a sullen burning glow like a kitchen range. The few passengers visible at mealtime—the majority had wearily dragged themselves ashore to explore the dubious pleasures of Bombay—took on the pallor of blanched peanuts. By sailing day, the pair of us were so comatose with ennui, so completely frustrated, exacerbated, and generally loco, that the event had lost its significance. The last we saw of India, sliding through the locks into the outer harbor, was a wizened beggar signaling us frantically for baksheesh. When none was forthcoming, he threw aside his servile manner and, bounding beside our porthole, dynamically thumbed his nose at us until we outdistanced him. It was a touching, and somehow an apt, symbol of the amity between our two great nations, and it made us proud that, within our limited capabilities, Hirschfeld and I had done our share to broaden and implement it.

Four days out, my stomach and the Arabian Sea arrived at a *modus vivendi;* it was agreed that the ocean would do its own heaving and my viscera the same. I made my way feebly to the dining room and, between sips of gruel, took inventory of our fellow-travelers. They were an unexciting lot. With a few colorful exceptions, like a family of Filipino mestizos, an Indian textile magnate and his wife, three nuns of the order of the Little Sisters of the Poor, and a Chinese insurance man, they were the sort of people you could have encountered at a New Jersey milk farm—prosperous, dowdy, fiercely normal. The quintet at our table, though, was not without a certain gargoyle charm.

Mrs. Kubic, a spirited, full-blown Latvian from Shanghai, was en route to Lausanne to place her adolescent daughter, Faustine, in school. At an age when most women are content to lay back on the oars, she was still as coquettish and full of wanton wiles as a sub-deb. In the presence of the opposite sex, her somewhat porcine face assumed the most terrifying ardor; she was continually directing languishing glances and melting smiles with lavish impartiality at the male passengers, deck stewards, officers, and foremast hands. The hoydenish Faustine, naturally, cramped her style a good deal, and her mother resorted to the most transparent devices to rid herself of the girl so she could exercise her blandishments. Mrs. Kubic's most winsome trait was an insistence on publicly airing her admiration for Hirschfeld's eyes in the poor chap's presence, likening them to those of a spaniel, and she succeeded in embarrassing him so completely that he kept them narrowed to mere slits whenever he ventured out of the cabin. The other lady at the table, a Mrs. Ledyard, was a flamboyant giantess in her fifties who owned a wire rope factory in Pawtucket, Rhode Island, and a roaring voice like the Bull of Bashan. Just why she was circumnavigating the globe she never made clear; the only time I noticed her display any particular enthusiasm was at Alexandria, when she caught sight of the rigging of a merchant ship near by. "Look!" she cried out jubilantly, seizing my arm in a paralyzing grip. "See that wire cable? It's our heavy-duty Number Three Tiger-Strand Special, Best by Test—isn't it a sweetheart?"

Flanking these personalities at the table were two men—Gruber, an energetic diamond importer with a sardonic manner and a huge store of information about the East, mainly inaccurate, and a quondam foreign correspondent named Ramspeck. Roger Ramspeck was a chubby, pompous youth who wore his hair aggressively *en brosse* and cultivated the air of tired condescension peculiar to the recipient of a Princeton sheepskin. For the preceding year he had been stationed in Nanking as representative of an obscure American news magazine, in which capacity he had unearthed some sublimely uninteresting facts about Chiang Kai-shek's boyhood. Ramspeck suffered from a common ailment of the immature; he would sit quiescent, brooding over Chiang's boyhood, then abruptly short-circuit the conversation with a remark so rude that it would focus everyone's attention on him. Our very first session together, he suddenly buried his face in his hands.

"Oh, God, how you all bore me!" he wailed. Mrs. Kubic and Mrs. Ledyard stared at him horrified, refusing to credit their ears.

"Ah, don't pay any attention to him," Gruber advised them, "he needs a good physic." Disregarding this excellent diagnosis, the ladies promptly and indignantly told Ramspeck his shortcomings.

To expose yourself
to the Egyptian border officials
is to invite certain apoplexy

He listened rapt, basking in their character analysis and drawing them on with piecemeal disclosures about his unhappy love life. It was obviously not the first time he had employed shock as a social gambit, and it was certainly not the last, for whenever the table talk showed signs of becoming adult, Ramspeck could always be depended on to wrench it toward himself. Before long, the rest of us gave up trying and contented ourselves with watching Ramspeck and Mrs. Kubic out-jockey each other for the egomania sweepstakes.

The heat, which had relaxed a trifle between India and Africa, redoubled the moment we raised the Straits of Bab el Mandeb and started into the Red Sea. Tongues lolling out, swollen with sunburn, we hung over the rail scanning the furnacelike profile of French Somaliland, surely the bleakest, most inhospitable coastline conceivable. Seven days' steaming from Bombay, we entered Port Tewfik, the harbor of Suez, and dropped anchor among the fleet of tankers lying there. Hirschfeld and I had subscribed, along with fourteen other passengers, for an overland tour to Cairo that would rejoin the ship at Alexandria after it cleared the Suez Canal. As soon as landing formalities were over—an interminable process of being chivvied by a couple of extremely bumbling, self-important, inefficient, and illiterate Egyptian shamuses—our group was ferried ashore and loaded into four sedans. It might be proper at this juncture to tender my respects to the Egyptian passport and customs service. Never, not even at the French *douane,* whose officiousness and pettifoggery are proverbial, have I beheld such egregious insolence and obstructionism. From the outset the wayfarer is treated to every possible humiliation a first-class bureaucracy can invent to bedevil him. He is assumed to be a gallows bird, a smuggler, and an anarchist, and is dealt with accordingly. To expose yourself to the Egyptian border official is to invite certain apoplexy; it is a source of constant surprise to me that I was able to emerge from the Nile Delta without blood on my hands. They can well hang their heads, these gentry—preferably on a row of pikes along the waterfront.

The trip across the desert to Cairo was as hot and exhausting as one would reasonably have supposed it to be in mid-July; a few skinny camels and the occasional rusted skeleton of an armored car or tank were the only objects visible in the stony, blinding waste.

The journey was made no shorter by the presence in our car of Mr. Kantharides, the travel agent who was playing Mother Carey to our flock of diversified chickens. He was a stout, oily gentleman, clearly hyperthyroid and possessed of what he considered to be fatal magnetism. He constantly kept kissing the ladies' hands, swapping heavy *double-entendres* with the men, and doing his utmost to promote the sort of sickly good-fellowship that prevails at a department-store clambake. The only person among us who ruffled his good nature was Mr. Chung, the Chinese insurance man. Chung, a very slow man with a piaster, convinced himself early in the jaunt that Kantharides was overcharging him and took to questioning each small expenditure.

"Six piasters for the lemon soda?" he demanded heatedly. "In Swatow we get a big bottle, twice the size of that one, for five cents!"

"It costs more here than in Swatow," snapped Kantharides. "What do you want, wholesale prices in the middle of the desert?"

"Ha-ha, you can't fool me," retorted Chung mockingly. "It all goes in your pocket. Look at that lunch we just had—thirty piasters. Why, in Swatow—"

"Swatow, Swatow!" screamed the infuriated Greek. "You're making me crazy with your Swatow! Why don't you go back there and drop dead?" He turned toward me, his face dark with passion, and I braced myself for a further outburst. Instead, in a perfectly matter-of-fact tone in which there was no trace of rancor, he remarked conversationally, "Some people just aren't reasonable, that's all."

Heliopolis, the great sprawling suburb of Cairo, sprang up unexpectedly around us in the fading dusk; there was something bizarre in these ornate villas and functional apartment houses blossoming without any preparation out of the arid plain. Bowling at breakneck speed past huge, crowded cafés and expensive shops, I felt for the first time the sense of Europe: the East was irretrievably behind us. It was not just the neon lights, the traffic, the purposefulness of the crowds on the boulevards, but a subtle acceleration of rhythm, the substitution of a wholly different scale of values. Our caravan drew up before the high terraced embankment of Shepheard's Hotel, and we straggled out on the sidewalk, parched, dusty, and irritable. Before we could stir a step, we were engulfed in a sea

In Swatow
we get a big bottle,
twice the size of that
one, for five cents

of dragomen, panders, peddlers, mendicants, fortunetellers, magicians, tumblers, fakirs, and assorted mountebanks, all screeching at the top of their voices. They trampled us, rent our clothing, showered us with beads, shawls, foul-smelling pocketbooks, swagger sticks, scarabs, horoscopes, alabaster funeral urns, and statuettes of Nefertiti, Horus, and Ammon Ra. Through their midst churned Kantharides, savagely boxing ears and calling down the most bloodthirsty imprecations. Slowly, inch by inch, hemmed in by a phalanx of porters garbed in fezzes and nightgowns and raining down gewgaws on the heads of our pursuers, we fought our way up to the hotel and safety.

In a late Victorian bedroom easily the size of the Hall of Mirrors at Versailles, furnished with gigantic brass bedsteads and papered a brooding crimson, Hirschfeld and I sprawled in the hot plush armchairs and caught our breath. A shred of sleazy muslin, torn from the burnoose of one of the importunate dragomen, dangled from the rim of my glasses; I disentangled it with the ponderous concentration of a man teetering on the edge of neurasthenia and let it drop. Together we watched it flutter dementedly to the floor. Then Hirschfeld expelled a deep, troubled sigh.

"Listen," he said, weighing every word, "this is a promise. If I ever get home again, I'm going to take every suitcase I own and burn it to ashes. Then I'm going to take a hammer and beat the ashes so that no --- -- - ----- can ever make a suitcase out of them again."

"Promise me one thing more," I said. "Don't throw away the hammer."

"Why?"

"Because," I said with equal deliberation, "if I ever suggest, if I ever so much as *hint* at, a trip anywhere, even Jersey City, I want you to take that hammer and beat me to a powder." Hirschfeld arose and extended his hand, his eyes shining.

"Old man," he said emotionally, "it'll be a pleasure."

Beads, shawls, foul-smelling pocketbooks, swagger sticks, scarabs, horo-
scopes, alabaster funeral urns, and statuettes of Nefertiti

10

Forty Centuries Look Down

THE CARBUNCULAR young Egyptian guide, his face lightly dappled with overexposure to the actinic ray and too many tourists, paused at the entrance of the passageway leading into the Great Pyramid at Gizeh and removed his fez. Extracting the monogrammed lawn handkerchief he had pilfered the day before from a wealthy Englishwoman, he unfolded it with excessive care, gave his forehead several dainty pats, tucked the handkerchief in his sleeve, and elegantly stifled a yawn. Without deigning to look at them, he knew that the three ancient attendants in the dirty white caftans, whose duty it was to conduct visitors through the maze of tunnels within, were watching him in respectful awe.

"What do you bring us today, our benefactor?" inquired one of the gaffers, lips skinned back over his gums in a particularly seductive smile.

"A bonanza, my father," returned the guide with self-satisfaction, "four nice pigeons ripe for the plucking—an Armenian, a Chinese, and two American journalists."

"In the name of Allah, effendi!" protested the old attendant, "are you insane? Who can get baksheesh out of an Armenian?"

"Pooh!" spat another, "the Armenian is a philanthropist compared to the Chinese!"

"And the two journalists are worse than either," moaned the third. "Those scavengers will end up stealing our turbans. Woe unto us, brothers—take to the hills!"

"Button your lip!" snapped the guide. "Here come the infidels now, and remember, whosoever among you tries to hold out on me in the final divvy, him will I beat with a besom until his noggin rings. Now bestir yourselves, loafers, for I hear *el moola* (the moola) jingling in their pockets." He darted away down the steps and, as Hirschfeld puffed into view at the head of our little sightseeing party, grasped his elbow solicitously and hoisted him up the last tier of masonry.

It was scarcely more than a couple of hours since sunup, but already the massive blocks of stone against which we leaned to regain our breath burned to the touch. The four of us—Chung, the Chinese insurance man, Hirschfeld, myself, and Wickwire, a malaria-ridden State Department employee from Siam whom our guide inexplicably persisted in regarding as a Levantine—had driven out from Cairo for a morning's rubbernecking with several other passengers from the *President Polk.* With infinitely sounder judgment than ourselves, however, the rest had elected to proceed immediately to the Sphinx rather than burrow into the recesses of the pyramids, and now, aboard a drove of mangy camels, were jolting off into the shimmering heat. An icy hand clutched my heart as I watched them go; some inner voice warned me to eschew this harebrained adventure while there was still time. Before I could summon up enough moxie to bolt after them, unfortunately, the attendants herded us into Indian file and nudged us forward. Stifling my panic by the simple expedient of biting off the tip of my tongue, I plunged into the chilling darkness.

The memory of the next half hour will haunt my dreams for years to come. Doubled over in a half crouch, we groped our way along a gallery approximately the length of the Simplon tunnel, crawled up a back-breaking ninety-degree incline studded with slippery metal cleats, and then, on all fours, scrambled everlastingly through a Stygian channel no bigger than a rain-barrel and certainly not as fragrant. Throughout the ordeal (purely to pass the time, of course), I amused myself with a number of quaint conceits: decided that the pyramid was slowly settling down on me, pretended I was buried alive, convinced myself an embolus was loose in my aorta and my extremities had turned to stone, and altogether managed to enrich every existing medical concept of claustrophobia. To add to my manifold problems, Mr. Chung, who was evidently in a state of keen anxiety also, clung to my ankles as we inched forward and lost consciousness from time to time, so that I was obliged to pull his weight as well as my own. At last, from up ahead, the exhilarating word was passed that we had gained our goal, and smeared with cobwebs, maimed, and grimy, we rolled into a small dank vault illuminated by the flares of the attendants.

"The Queen's Chamber, gents," panted Hassan, our guide. "Very old." We stood about staring vacuously at the very old premises for a moment, hungering for an epochal revelation about its significance, but apparently Bubastis, the sacred cat, had Hassan's tongue. Finally he broke the painful silence with a discreet cough. "Excuse me, noble sirs, but I think the boys would like a little baksheesh."

"Oh, they would, would they?" rejoined Hirschfeld belligerently. "And what cooks if we don't give them any?"

"I think," said Hassan with a feline grin, "that it would be much sooner to get out if you did." I do not recall ever having heard a remark which carried so many interesting implications, and since the four of us were men of quick understanding, we grasped them all in a flash. Personally, I would have loved to spend the winter creeping through the complex network of passages and exploring the balance of the sarcophagi, but it would have been selfish to let personal considerations detain the other members of the party, and swallowing my chagrin, I promptly whacked up my share of the pay-off. We completed the return journey in jig time; some mysterious metamorphosis in the royal tomb had endowed me with the agility of a lizard, for I was out of the pyramid and gasping on the sand a full five minutes before Hirschfeld, Chung, and Wickwire emerged. Beyond the fact that we were breathing, the affair had only one compensating aspect—our guide's Promethean fury when he discovered that his new ball-point fountain pen, which he had been exhibiting pridefully all morning, had been heisted by the attendants. Taking advantage of the hullabaloo of splintered Arabic and heartrending lamentations that ensued, we hastily chartered a panel of burros and galloped off smartly to the Sphinx. The howl of the hyena is supposed to be the eeriest sound in the Libyan Desert, but I will match it with Hassan's scream of anguish as he realized that our donkey-boys had flimflammed him out of a fee.

There are, no doubt, individuals of such shining stoicism that they can stand face to face with the Sphinx in a July noonday sun, with the thermometer at 119 Fahrenheit and a plague of sand-flies assailing them, and derive from it the intellectual catharsis it is said to produce. I wish that I were one of them. As it was, all I bore away from the encounter was a nose burned the color of an eggplant and a fearsome case of bloat induced by drinking seven bottles of soda pop in quick succession. Some anonymous genius has had the inspiration to pitch a soft-drink stand a few hundred feet away, or possibly it was even part of the original statue; in any case, I never expect to recapture the gratitude I felt for that pitiful patch of shade. The next morning there arrived at the hotel a photograph of two goatish imbeciles, each mounted on a dromedary in front of a pyramid with his arm encircling the bust of a lady passenger, which the dragoman insisted Hirschfeld and I had posed for. It was sheer blackmail, naturally, because apart from the coincidence that the spalpeens were wearing our faces and clothes, they were quite dissimilar; but rather than create a fuss, we slipped the wretch a couple of thousand piasters, threatened to blacken his eye if he ever mentioned it, and sank the photograph in the Nile.

The tourist who hopes to get any valid impression of Cairo from a thirty-six-hour stay is, to put it mildly, fatuous, and the program of activities designed for us by Mr. Kantharides, our conductor, played heavily on this gullibility. By nightfall we had been hustled at dizzying speed through the Blue Mosque, the bazaars, the National Museum, and a score of jewelry shops we were positive the wily Greek operated under a multiplicity of assumed names. Any rational citizen would have had the grace to collapse after so punishing a day, but Hirschfeld and I had reached the stage of hypertension that recognizes no fatigue. Whipping into fresh tarbooshes, we

125

charged off to an open-air vaudeville establishment to witness a celebrated muscle-dancer named Badia who was currently, so to speak, holding Cairo in the hollow of her navel. The lady was unquestionably gifted, as is anyone who can keep an audience of two thousand art-lovers enthralled with a repetition of the same basic pattern, yet there were moments, along about three-thirty in the morning, when one's attention flagged. Hirschfeld likewise noticed that our whistles and erotic moans were losing their first intensity; and ordering an usher to convey a floral horseshoe to the star (for which, stupidly enough, we neglected to give him the money), we sleepily wended our way back to Shepheard's.

At three o'clock the following afternoon, had you been dawdling around the ocean front at Alexandria ninety miles to the north, you would have glimpsed a scene to bring tears to the most jaundiced eye. My colleague and I, still streaked with coal-dust accumulated on the rigorous rail trip up from Cairo, were draped over a table in the Café Athenaeos, having just annihilated a quart of pistachio ice cream, four chocolate éclairs, three charlotte russes, and a little assorted pastry. A cool, delicious Mediterranean breeze ruffled our hair and fanned our fevered cheeks; no words can convey the measure of utter, blissful well-being that pervaded us. I am not at all sure our stomachs could have withstood a diet of pure carbohydrate longer than the few hours we luxuriated waiting for our steamer, but to nervous systems frazzled from months of tropical heat, the city seemed almost paradisiacal. Its people were cordial and colorful, its atmosphere civilized, and its climate soothing, and if anyone is disposed to link my name with the Alexandria Chamber of Commerce, he has another link coming. I am in love with a certain Mediterranean seaport and I don't care who knows it.

In the couple of days it took the *President Polk* to cover the distance between Alexandria and Naples, the passengers' spirits underwent a marked change. The idyllic weather and the exciting proximity of Europe generated a vigor and bonhomie that had been hitherto lacking; even I found myself showing a hundred little unaccustomed kindnesses, like presenting the purser with a box of wormy figs I had purchased from a leper in Colombo or refusing to

127

read Hirschfeld's personal mail when he left it indiscreetly strewn about the cabin. The captain's dinner, the night preceding our arrival in Italy, aroused the strain of relentless whimsy latent in ocean travelers the world over. Eleven persons turned up dressed as sheikhs, and practically every female on board, except the stewardess and several old harridans too sunk in apathy to care, came as Oulëd Naïl girls. Mrs. Ledyard, the Amazon at our table who owned the wire cable factory in Rhode Island, felt it best to wear on her head an old-fashioned, befringed parlor lamp-shade. How she procured it nobody knew, and I can only infer that she must have portaged it all the way from Pawtucket for just such an occasion. At one point in the saturnalia, when the fun was at its grimmest, Mrs. Ledyard suddenly gave way to an excess of animal energy. She caught up a springy iron clapper, and, since I am always in the trajectory of people like that, fetched me a lethal blow on the sconce, causing a goose-egg. I overlooked it at the time, realizing the woman was in wine, but my salutation thereafter was the frostiest of nods and I suspect she gathered she had breached the canons of good taste.

It did not require an especially perceptive nature to sense from the moment we tied up at Naples the sadness and dilapidation of the city. Great stretches of dockside and industrial district were still in ruins, and the population, or what remnant was visible in the echoing, poorly lighted streets, seemed malnourished and despairing. Perhaps it was this heavy oppressiveness, aggravated by the rumor that the ship might be detained there, that stampeded me into joining the excursion I did. If I had suspected its true scope, or the complete naïveté of trying to cover a major portion of Italy in four days, I might have harkened to Hirschfeld and sailed with him to Genoa. But then, that would have been sagacious, and sagacity has never been my long suit.

On the surface, to one who had never been in the country, our itinerary appeared perfectly feasible—Pompeii, Rome, Siena, Florence, Pisa, and on to Genoa by the Italian Riviera. In the big red Fiat bus with me that sparkling morning went eight other innocents —Wickwire and Chung, the intrepid duo who had helped me solve the riddle of the Great Pyramid; Mr. Sabadhai, a pursy Indian textile magnate, and his wife; Azeez, a sniveling young Bengali on his way to Johns Hopkins to study dentistry; the Beavers, a well-heeled elderly couple from Lake Forest; and Miss Gorsline, a spinsterish New England schoolteacher. In charge of the flock, and none too elated with his assignment, was a peppery, disenchanted Neapolitan named Mr. Frascati, whose expression of choler hardly deserted him from the instant he saw us. He considered the expedition unmitigated lunar idiocy, and I must say nothing happened to disprove him.

We tore through Pompeii in a dog-trot, frantically snatching postcards and marveling dutifully at the reconstructions; anyone who showed a tendency to browse was quickly shooed along by Frascati, who made it clear the schedule allowed no time for giggling over erotica. By midday we were boiling through the Apennine hill towns at a terrifying rate, in our wake a series of moribund chickens and peasants screaming maledictions. The scenery was spectacular: endless rolling vineyards under full cultivation, medieval villages perched on the most outlandish crags, superb perspectives of cypresses and Lombardy poplars outlined against the sky. At Viterbo, a somnolent mountain hamlet out of a Shubert operetta, we dallied long enough to gulp down a flask of memorable white wine and allow a bullock to trample on my foot and thundered on. The havoc caused by bombs and shellfire, sporadic until now, became truly appalling at the Volturno. The destruction was so overwhelming that you wondered how men found the courage to face the task of rebuilding; and yet there, as everywhere along the Via Appia, were constant evidences of a tenacious, energetic rehabilitation. No monument or shrine I saw in central Italy, and I was fated to see nearly all of them, was half as impressive as the dogged industry with which the people were restoring their homes and workshops.

There is a pungent old Calabrian proverb, whose meaning I have forgotten if I ever knew it, which states that the human spinal column can stand a powerful lot of abuse. Mine certainly served as a whipping boy that day. Long after dark, spent and nerve-weary, I doddered into the foyer of a third-rate hotel in Rome, was fed as wretched a meal of rubbery veal and warmed-over spaghetti as a swindling management could confect on short notice, and was bivouacked in a disused storeroom. My slumber was a mite less than refreshing; Azeez, my Indian bunkmate, dreamt he was being crushed by the Juggernaut and howled like a timber wolf all night long. The next morning found us on the treadmill in earnest; paced by Frascati, we sprinted through the mile-long corridors of the Vatican, gaped at Michelangelo's murals in the Sistine Chapel, goggled at the immensity of St. Peter's. After lunch, Wickwire and I made a desperate attempt to vamoose, but the guide had been ordered to show us Rome and show it he did. Blubbering and begging for mercy, we were haled to the Borghese Gardens, the Roman Forum, the Colosseum, the Piazza Venezia, and the gigantic cheese fondant commemorating Victor Emmanuel. Somewhere in the midst of these architectural glories, my feet ceased to function as organs of locomotion and I finished the day *hors de combat*, numbly festooned over Frascati and Wickwire in the humiliating posture known as the fireman's carry. With admirable presence of mind, they dragged me to a small surgery on the Corso, where my jaws were pried open with a sharp stick and a shakerful of martinis introduced, and soon I was reeling back to my hotel, yodeling *La Traviata* as good as new.

It would serve no useful purpose to prolong the agonizing chronicle of our hegira; once established, the hallucinatory pattern intensified like that of a six-day bicycle race. Out of the nightmare I remember isolated highlights: a truly symphonic dish of green noodles in Siena, the panorama of Tuscan hills that was purest primitive painting, the theatrical splendor of Florence, the breathtaking Byzantine mosaics in the cathedral at Pisa, a lunch deserving of the Cordon Bleu in a tiny restaurant in Viareggio. Interthreaded through it is the recollection of unending heat and dust, of a blurred succession of churches, fountains, and largely hideous sculpture, and the tireless clack of Miss Gorsline's tongue as she annotated the wonders whirling by us. When we reached the Italian Riviera at last, the driver cast discretion to the winds and decided to give us

a farewell *frisson*. All his southern Latin daredeviltry rose to the surface; throttle wide open, rocking and careering around horrid chasms, the bus hurtled down the precipitous coast past La Spezia and Rapallo as though Beelzebub himself were at the controls. Our homecoming created a minor sensation aboard the *President Polk* and provided touching proof, if any was necessary, of the esteem our mates felt for us. So sure had everyone been that we would never return alive that our effects had been auctioned off among the passengers. I consumed a whole day retrieving my wardrobe from other people's cabins and had many piquant adventures, none of them, however, pertinent to this narrative.

The lights of Genoa were vanishing astern that evening as Hirschfeld and I, languidly brushing from our cummerbunds the crumbs of our final dinner aboard the *Polk*, sauntered out on the promenade deck. In the afterglow of the sunset the Mediterranean was dark

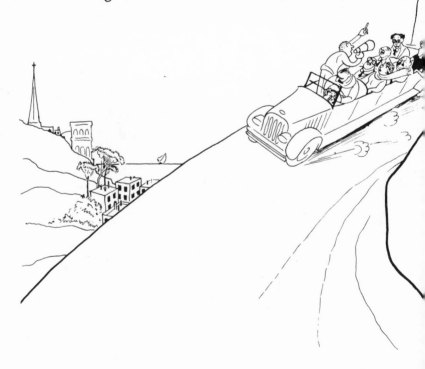

and smoothly rippling; off on the horizon ahead, the faint jagged sil-
houette of the Côte d'Azur was fast taking shape. It was the poetic
hour of twilight, the hushed diminuendo that concludes every
FitzPatrick Traveltalk, and it cried out for some cosmic reflection
that would sum up man's tangled destiny and the quintessence of
everything we had experienced thus far. Ever more attuned to the
infinite than myself, Hirschfeld was the first to put it into words.

"It's a rum thing," he observed thoughtfully, "but in all the thousands of miles I've traveled and all the books I've read, I never
heard of anybody catching beriberi in the Sixth Avenue Deli-
catessen."

"Come, come, man," I objected, "don't be an ingrate! Think of
the people who'd like to be in your shoes right now."

"I am," he muttered, "and they're for rent from here in. Oh, well,"
he shrugged, flinging away his cheroot in a wide curving arc, "this
trip's taught me one lesson anyway. You can't have your strüdel
and eat it too. See you in France." And he went below.

11

Seamy Side Up

ON A SWELTERING Sunday evening in the closing days of July, the sleek reception clerk of the Hôtel Negresco in Nice looked up from his ledger and beheld, approaching him across the lobby, a grotesque duo. Offhand, it appeared to be a team of tramp comedians, except that the make-up and costumes of the pair were, if anything, a shade too broad. The bearded half of the act, a villainous customer on the order of Mack Swain, was clad in a military raincoat, baby-blue shorts, shrunken white socks, and open-toed sandals. The other, bespectacled and snaffle-toothed, nervously scratching a chin you could hang a lantern on, wore a white twill fisherman's hat, a greasy bush jacket, khaki bathing trunks, and a pair of scuffies. A clerk with less aplomb might have yielded to a pardonable impulse to snatch up the cashbox, sound the alarm, and hide in the lavabo until the gendarmes came. Two considerations, however, gave this one pause: first, he had just received an excited phone call from the stationmaster, employing the Provençal word "halvies," informing him that a brace of eccentric American millionaires had tumbled off the Marseilles express, and second, his X-ray eye, trained to pick out a dead beat under the most flawless dinner coat, unerringly diagnosed the bulge in the gentlemen's waistbands as American Express checks. By the time, consequently, that the bearded type had begun identifying himself in the execrable French accent that had flunked him out of Principia High School in St. Louis, the clerk was way ahead of him.

"*Mais certainement, mon cher M. Hirschfeld!*" he cooed, vaulting over the desk and pinching our money-belts playfully. "The royal suite, the grand ballroom, the moon if you like! Jacques! Étienne! Carry in the baggage—and gently with that typewriter, idiot, don't you know platinum when you see it?" While we toiled over the police questionnaires, our Boniface smacked his lips over the room chart. Yes, he could let us share the fifth floor with the Nizam of Hyderabad, though man to man, he ought to warn us that facilities for mooring a yacht there were limited. His own recommendation was that we book the three top floors favored by the Aga Khan, unless, of course, we minded stabling our horses in the bridal suite. Eventually, we plucked the opium pipe from his teeth and brusquely demanded a double room and bath. The descent to reality was so abrupt that it left him speechless for an instant. As we shot skyward in the lift five minutes later, I could still hear him shrilly bombinating to the head porter. "Fakers, tin-horn sports!" he was choking. "I saw right through them, but *nom de Dieu,* what could I do? They held a gun against my ribs!"

Conditioned as we were to the noisome rabbit warrens that masquerade as hotel rooms in the East, our bedchamber at the Negresco seemed like heaven on the half shell. Granted the décor was pure marzipan, a riot of rosebuds, pink taffeta, and gilt; notwithstanding, there were real box springs, a bathtub big enough to float an LST, an infinity of towels. When we finally descended into the Promenade des Anglais for an aperitif, no feminine heads swiveled around to exclaim at our comeliness, but at least we had the merit of being reasonably clean. Fortified by a few Cinzanos, we sat at a café table on the esplanade and watched the vacation crowd undulating past. It had the same opulent, *sportif* air I remembered from my last visit thirteen years before, and yet I became increasingly aware of a profound change. Everyone was much more subdued; I saw little evidence of the effervescence, the explosive arguments, the gesticulation, and the exaggerated passion of old.

People's appearance, too, had undergone a definite transformation. Every other woman was a chemical blonde resolutely modeling herself on Veronica Lake or Lauren Bacall, and the men's clothes were indistinguishable from those on Mosholu Parkway and Michi-

Naughty but nice: the Boulevard des Anglais

gan Boulevard. Probably the most distressing note in the scene to a couple of Francophiles was the prevalence of the American ice-cream cone. Baby, dowager, gigolo, and slippered pantaloon, all the world and his wife had their noses plunged in some form of popsicle or candied apple as they passed in review before us. We both understood to what depths France had sunk when a Chevalier of the Legion of Honor, sporting a monocle and a white imperial, trotted by munching an Eskimo Pie. Had Marcel Proust suddenly materialized with a mouthful of bubble gum, we could not have been more deeply disenchanted. "That tears it," snapped Hirschfeld, rising in disgust. "Come on, let's have dinner—and the way our luck is running, I bet it'll be corned beef hash."

His fears were superfluous; the meal proved to be magnificent, a work of such consummate artistry that it even assuaged the shock of the bill when it arrived. Perhaps two bottles of Beaune '23 and a demijohn of Calvados also helped to cushion the blow; in any case, we teetered out into the night airily impervious to the fact that we had pauperized ourselves in a single stroke. The ensuing events are a bit kaleidoscopic. I recall whirling along the Middle Corniche road in a rented Panhard-Levassor that must have steered itself, since the driver was seated with us in the tonneau harmonizing "Auprès de Ma Blonde." Superimposed on this are three or four zigzag flashes, technically akin to what are termed Vorkapich shots in Hollywood, of the Casino at Monte Carlo: a fiendish wooden rake darting at me like an adder and decimating my stack of counters; a vinegary cashier with the face of a bluebottle fly spurning my wrist watch as if it were infected; a short interregnum of Greco-Roman wrestling with a doorman; and the springy recoil of a privet hedge as I soared over a white marble balustrade and bounced into it. Evidently, however, one of us must have performed some act of gallantry deserving of public acclaim, because when I came back into focus, we were in a *boite* called the Club Maxim receiving an ovation from a bevy of charming young maidens. We all seemed to be on a footing of the greatest cordiality. Hirschfeld, wearing one of the ladies' hats, was demonstrating his proficiency at the can-can, and I was serenading the company with an instrument on which I am some-

thing of a virtuoso, a piece of tissue paper stretched over a comb.

Never, I venture to say, has jollity been so spontaneous and unrehearsed, but it was getting late, and anxious not to disrupt the party, we essayed to steal out quietly through the kitchen. We learned then and there that you do not lightly flout the laws of French hospitality. With many good-natured sallies and a firm grasp on our coat collars, the manager escorted us back and presented us with a souvenir document solemnizing the occasion. I forget its exact wording, but after we finished acknowledging it, our throats were dry and our dependents doomed. It still hangs over the bar at Maxim's, framed as neatly as the manager knows how, and he certainly knows how.

At the end of forty-eight hours in Nice, our arteries and our resources were too brittle to withstand added stress, and ruthlessly deafening our ears to the siren song of the Midi, we struck out for Paris. We began to get an inkling of what conditions there might be from the dinner served en route in the Wagon-Lits restaurant. The roast (a purely formal designation) was microscopic, the vegetables a travesty, the bread well-nigh inedible, sugar, cream, and butter nonexistent—and this aboard a luxury train which before the war had prided itself on its posh cuisine. Another contrast to the good old days greeted us on disembarking at the Gare de Lyon the following morning. Instead of the crowd of importunate taxidrivers we expected, there was a queue of travelers a block long wrangling like fishwives for the infrequent cab that loitered by. Excluding pots, pans, and a tent, my colleague and I had managed in seven months' wandering to accumulate more gear than a gypsy caravan; and since we had thoughtlessly forgotten to stock a Conestoga wagon, we could think of no feasible way of spanning the five miles to our Left Bank hotel. Ultimately, we made it in tortuous, roundabout fashion through the subway, aided by four porters groaning in the best safari tradition. We all became fast friends in the process, and to show their esteem, the men put on an impromptu decathlon in the lobby which consisted of beating their heads on the floor, kicking the luggage, and jumping up and down on our tips.

The character exists, unquestionably, who managed to have a rip-roaring time in Paris in the summer of 1947, but who he is, where he did so, and how he found the inclination, I cannot imagine. To my way of thinking, it was one of the more woeful locales west of Shanghai; the food scarcity was acute, the cost of living was astronomical, and a pall of futility and cynicism hung over the inhabitants. Physically, to be sure, the city was completely unchanged; it was still the most beautiful capital on earth, but it was mere architecture, a series of superb vistas forsaken by the spirit that had once animated it. There were streets, indeed, whole quarters, devoid of any sign of life and business appeared to be at a complete standstill. Everywhere you went, you sensed the apathy and bitterness of a people corroded by years of enemy occupation.

Under these melancholy circumstances, therefore, it may be appreciated why the lengthy visit we had projected soon shrank to the dimensions of a condolence call. Out of some dim feeling of obligation, we forced ourselves back to the cafés and restaurants we had frequented in the spacious Twenties, only to reaffirm that there are far cheerier pastimes than lingering in a haunted house. After ten o'clock in Montparnasse, which used to be a fairly boisterous parish, the prairie dogs came out of their holes; Montmartre was not half as iniquitous as Barnegat, New Jersey, and considerably less charged with glamour. The Café Flore, popularized by Jean-Paul Sartre and the Existentialist coterie, drew together on its terrace a few unreconstructed Bohemians, but the only procurable drinks, synthetic grape juice and venomous French beer, did not make for vivacity or sparkle. Food was the constant preoccupation and, with the majority of persons we met, the sole topic of conversation; the American tourist like ourselves, who symbolized prosperity and whose dollars ruled the world economy, was popularly regarded as either a pigeon or a usurer. Altogether, the atmosphere was every whit as cheerless and unnerving as our previous information had described it; and it was with a sensation of exquisite relief that we finally threw in the sponge and entrained for London. I had never felt that way before in leaving Paris, and I experienced a twinge of guilt that it should be possible. But this was not the city I had known and

141

really loved—it was a jarring echo out of the past, a brief, disturbing episode I hoped to subordinate to rosier memories.

The Channel crossing, a chore even under optimum conditions, was aggravated in my case by an unforeseen affliction, a heroic-sized plaster cast of the head of Buddha I was toting home to supplement the windy after-dinner discourses I planned. I had acquired it in Paris; it was not a very good head, but it cost only four dollars, which in my muddled logic conclusively branded it a bargain. Done up in brown manila paper in typically slapdash French fashion, it made a package about the size of a flexible flyer. Early in the trip, I convinced myself that someone would accidentally shatter it, so, hugging it fearfully to my breast, I sat bolt upright all the way to Calais, sweating with panic each time the railway carriage lurched. To increase my agitation, the bundle seemed to possess a strange magnetic attraction for the other passengers, who constantly kept ricocheting into it, hooking it with their umbrellas, and generally trying to demolish it. An appeal to their aesthetic sensibilities went for naught; various coarse innuendoes were ad-

The Café Flore, popularized by Jean-Paul Sartre and the Existentialist coterie, drew together on its terrace a few unreconstructed Bohemians

143

vanced, that I was disposing of an unwelcome mistress, trafficking in white slaves, smuggling cocaine, and so on. Fortunately for my equilibrium, the wretched thing disappeared somewhere on the Channel steamer, for had I had to play governess to a bagful of plaster the balance of the journey, there might well have been psychiatric repercussions.

If anybody would like a few facile platitudes about the English people from a man who spent twelve days in London, I have the largest stock of new and used generalizations in the business. They have two qualities in common: they are all glib and all equally shallow. With minor variations, they are the same fatuities an Englishman who has spent twelve days in New York would spout. Nevertheless, there were a couple of traits I observed often enough in my stay to believe that they must be basic national character-istics: courage and serenity. It needed plenty of both to have en-dured the rigors of the foregoing seven years and to face an extremely dubious future, and that they were still apparent struck me as nothing short of a miracle. Perhaps, coming from the despair and lethargy of Paris, the contrast was especially keen, but from the glimpse of postwar London I had, my admiration for British forti-tude was unbounded.

There is an infallible test for detecting a tourist in any metropolis in the world—simply look for a man standing in front of a cutlery or luggage shop with his mouth ajar, gazing vacantly in at the manicure sets, razor strops, and collar-boxes and jingling the change in his pockets. Nine times out of ten, investigation will prove he hails from some point outside the city limits, be it Yakima, Nairobi, or Antofagasta. Hirschfeld and I adhered faithfully to the classic tradition, except that we broadened it to include every tobacco-nist's, bookstore, haberdashery, tailoring establishment, and boot-maker's in the West End. Before we wrote finis to a week of shopping, we had successfully slimmed down our purses to the vanishing point and amassed a weird profusion of phony Stafford-shire, shooting sticks, brandy decanters, hand-tied flies suitable for whipping the streams off Times Square, tab-collar shirts that pinched our throats, and underslung pipes we had no intention of

A comedienne named Hermione Gingold, whose style may be loosely described as an amalgam of Groucho Marx and Tallulah Bankhead

smoking. In a burst of affection, we also picked up a few paltry gifts for our families: tweed coats for our small daughters that would have fitted a Grenadier guardsman, a blow-gun with poisoned darts for my son, and some enchanting limp-leather diaries for our wives in which to jot down the household expenses. The latter, to be sure, was just a munificent gesture on our part, as neither of the girls, Lord love them, had ever learned to write, but we figured it was the sentiment rather than the keepsake that mattered.

London after dark we found to be on the whole not much more beguiling than Paris, although the theater was flourishing and, if you could readjust yourself to a curtain that rose at six-thirty, providing some brisk diversions. The outstanding, to our taste, was a revue starring a comedienne named Hermione Gingold, whose style may be loosely described as an amalgam of that of Groucho Marx and Tallulah Bankhead. Seen from the aisles where we rolled about freely on the three occasions we attended, the lady impressed us as the wittiest and most engaging performer in many a year. Her touch was consistently dextrous, whether she was depicting a musical comedy favorite of the 1900's, an elderly clublady delivering a dissertation on India, or the hapless subject of a cubist portrait painter. Following our last visit, we paid homage to her in her dressing room; I made a long, fervent address crammed with superlatives, enjoining her to do with our hearts as she saw fit. She was plainly overcome—blushed the color of a peony, modestly cast down her eyes, bathed us in ardent glances, and made repeated attempts to staunch my flow of eloquence. I learned later from a reliable source named Hirschfeld that Cary Grant had been standing directly behind me vainly trying to proffer his compliments, but I like to think they must have seemed pretty wooden after mine. That is what I like to think, and hell's bells, a man can think what he likes.

The thorniest problem we faced in London, and one that taxed our ingenuity to unravel, was the staggering cultural program we had outlined for ourselves, how to crowd a wealth of symphony concerts, art exhibits, and historic sites into the period preceding our sailing. We solved it in a rather effective manner, if I do say so, by merely tearing up the list we had prepared. We did, though, devote a morning to two places of prime aesthetic significance, Madame Tussaud's waxworks and Sherlock Holmes's chambers in Baker Street.

At the former, I had a trifling contretemps that robbed me of my appetite for a day or so; in the dimly lit Chamber of Horrors, I linked arms with a bearded party I supposed to be Hirschfeld and discovered somewhat belatedly that it was Henri Landru. Unluckily, a button on my sleeve got entangled in the manikin's vest, and by the time we were sorted out, Landru and my poise were in shreds. At 122-b Baker Street, we were dismayed to see that a grocery store occupied the great detective's diggings. The four stolid clerks insisted that nobody named Holmes had ever lived there. I maintained hotly that he, or rather his fictional self, most definitely had and, treating them to a scathing lecture on their ignorance, stormed out. Of course, I knew all along that Holmes's correct address was 221-b, as Hirschfeld triumphantly pointed out on checking up; I was only testing the clerks to puncture their middle-class smugness. It really astonishes one, traveling about the globe, to learn how little comprehension people have of their own literary background.

That a jubilee spirit hovered over one spot in London I can vouch for, and that was the platform at Waterloo Station the afternoon we caught the boat train for Southampton. The homeward-bound Americans were as merry as grigs (the Southern Railway had considerately furnished a box of grigs for purposes of comparison), and the English passengers were dewy-eyed with anticipation of the victuals awaiting them on the *Queen Mary*. Every man in sight had a brand-new suit of Glen Urquhart plaid and a pigskin attaché case, twirled a cane bright with varnish, and puffed on a shiny brier; the womenfolk, parading those dove-gray tailleurs and fur-pieces they invariably don for the shortest train jump, were entwined with orchids. For our part, Hirschfeld and I betrayed not the slightest exuberance at leave-taking, beyond an occasional handspring or a shrill Comanche war whoop. The fact that we abandoned the train halfway and sprinted ahead, beating it into Southampton by half an hour, also meant nothing; we just felt the need for a bit of healthful exercise. I guess it was when my friend proposed that we by-pass the steamer and swim to Newfoundland that I really began to suspect we were returning in the nick of time. But then, any fool could have told us as much—that is, any fool who could read a letter of credit.

12

Home Is the Hunted

SILHOUETTED against the afterglow of the fiery red sun which had vanished a moment before over the mid-Atlantic horizon, the chief officer of the *Queen Mary* paced the bridge, frowning into the gathering darkness. From the deck beneath his feet came the even, measured throb of the ship's pulse as she cleft the trackless deep, driving ever onward toward the shores of the New World. It had been a halcyon day; wind and water were favoring the voyage, passengers and crew alike were in a frame of high good humor, and all indications pointed to a smooth, uneventful run to Ambrose Channel sixty hours distant. And yet this vigilant watcher of the skies, on whose shoulders rested the responsibility for the leviathan and her cargo of four thousand souls, was oppressed by a vague disquiet. A feeling of remissness, as of some major obligation neglected, gnawed his conscience. Again and again he grappled with it, seeking to ferret out its source, but try as he would, the reason eluded him. At last, with a sigh of frustration, he threw open the door of the chartroom, entered, and addressed the young officer hunched over a set of calipers.

"Look here, ffoulis," he said abruptly, "a feeling of remissness, as of some major obligation neglected, has been gnawing my conscience. Can you give me any clue to this vague disquiet?"

"Why, yes, sir," said ffoulis, whose business it was to know everything, "perhaps it concerns that colorful pair of birds in Cabin 541 which their cognomens are Hirschfeld and Perelman and which they have for the last eight months been running the gamut of exotic climes from the frozen barrens of Manchuria to the sun-baked delta of the Nile."

"By Jove—of course!" exploded his senior. "Wonderful chaps—salt of the earth! I meant to have a drink with them, but I was too busy out there having my conscience gnawed. Tell me: has any stone been left unturned to provide for their animal comfort whilst aboard this here microcosm?"

"No, indeed, sir," said the other, "their fastidious palates have been tickled with our choicest viands, their tongues loosened with our rarest vintages, and their ears regaled with our most lilting dance harmonies."

"In short," nodded the chief, "they have been living like pigs in clover."

"I don't know about the clover part," admitted ffoulis, "but believe me, chief—"

"That will do, ffoulis," the chief interrupted sternly. "Where are these two arresting personalities at this instant?"

"Where they usually are," said the young man, "in the Pompeian bar getting fractured on Manhattans."

"Then we need not addle our pates anent them," said the chief, picking up the calipers and unfurling a map. "Come, let us put the chart before the course." And he fell to work with a will.

Actually, the junior's surmise as to our whereabouts was mistaken; at the moment we were seated in the ship's lounge in a state of dreamy absorption, listening to a string ensemble sawing Cécile Chaminade in half and wondering why we felt like a couple of characters in *Outward Bound*. For there was a definitely eerie quality about the vast salon with its glaring candelabra, its ghostly creak of woodwork, and its half-dozen cardiac cases slumbering in the overstuffed furniture. The stewards flitted soundlessly over the thick carpets, and frequently, when they passed between us and the light, a faint ectoplasmic glow seemed to outline their forms. Any minute you expected a grave but kindly messenger, impersonated by Edward Everett Horton or Claude Rains, to materialize to the muted sound of bells and beckon you into the hereafter.

The same sense of unreality, of other-worldliness, had in fact obsessed us ever since embarking on the *Mary* two days before at Southampton. Lost in her sheer magnitude, submerged in the endless swarms of passengers circulating through her myriad smoking rooms, restaurants, shopping galleries, verandas, and foyers, we found ourselves assuming an anonymous, wraithlike aspect. Our conversation was pitched in whispers and our normal gait slowed to a shuffle; we reported obediently at meals, queued up at the merest tinkle of a gong, salaamed in the most servile fashion to anyone wearing a wisp of gold braid. From the labels on our luggage and the occasional whiff of salt air that penetrated our porthole, we were dimly aware that we were at sea, but every artful device of modern hotel management had been employed to insulate us. Our cabin, a luxurious affair in brown and beige, was a marvel of compression, elevators inlaid in semi-precious stones whisked us from keel to topmast, and a host of barbers, tailors, masseurs, trainers, couriers, and assorted lackeys trembled at our whim. It was hemispheric travel on its loftiest level, and, to a couple of peasants like Hirschfeld and myself, unaccustomed to such splendors, a wholly spectral experience.

It was made even more so by the appearance at our table of a brace of citizens, Cozine by name, bizarre enough to unhinge the strongest reason. Wallace Cozine was a sallow, rumpled individual in tweeds and a pale red beard who modestly confessed at our only luncheon together that he was perhaps the world's foremost surrealist photographer. He and his wife, a gaunt, cavernous-eyed creature laden with quantities of abstract costume jewelry, had been visiting Paris the previous month in behalf of a small advance-guard magazine called *Umlaut!*, and there was no phase of French culture, politics, or cuisine they were not equipped to discuss in exhaustive detail and with absolute authority. It was obvious from the start that they had conceived a very low opinion of our taste, and they could not comprehend how we had passed through France without meeting the people who were doing the really challenging things.

"Who did you see there?" demanded Cozine. "Did you see Hans Raffia?"

"Who's that?" asked Hirschfeld.

"You mean to tell me you never heard of Hans Raffia?" hooted Cozine. "Why, the man's ceramics have practically revolutionized the whole conception of modern art!"

"We—er—we didn't get to look at much crockery," I faltered.

"Anybody who calls ceramics crockery is a boob, a barbarian, and a Yahoo," announced Cozine in a voice audible across the dining room. We accepted the classification with submissive smiles and pretended to be engrossed in our chicken patties. After a pause, his wife resumed the inquisition.

"What about Stanislaus Farkas?" she probed. "Did you see his show of non-objective horseshoes at the Galérie Frugl?"

"We . . . got there right after it closed," said Hirschfeld lamely. "The director was just putting up the shutters—"

"Aha," murmured Cozine cynically, "and I don't suppose you saw Serge Smetana's invisible ballet either."

"How could we if it was invisible?" I protested. "I mean—"

"*Nothing's* invisible unless you close your mind to it," snapped Cozine, "but of course you couldn't have seen Smetana—he didn't give any recitals at the American Express Company." By the conclusion of the meal, they had so effectively demolished our self-esteem that we slunk off to the stateroom and thereafter had our food sent in on a tray. A day or two later, an envelope containing a picture postcard of the Eiffel Tower was slipped surreptitiously under the door. "Thought you'd like this," the note with it read. "Maybe it'll convince *somebody* you were in Paris, even if we don't think so." There was no clue to the sender, but the left-hand corner of the envelope bore the crisp legend "Umlaut! A Lance to Puncture Hypocrisy and Sham."

On the fourth morning, a new air of energy and purposefulness animated the ship; the bulletin boards bloomed with landing instructions, batteries of fountain pens scratched away at customs declarations, mountains of trunks choked the promenade decks. Caught up in the universal hysteria of homecoming, we pelted through the shops buying last-minute gifts that duplicated ones we already had and feverishly sent off dramatic cablegrams announcing our advent to families long oppressed by the fact. Then, loins girded, we attacked the job of winnowing from our baggage the exotic chaff the experts had insisted we take on the tour. Out through the porthole went the glass beads, red cloth, and Mother Hubbards we had planned to trade to savage tribes. After them went the maps of Tasmania, the Swahili dictionaries, the collapsible drinking cups, the Primus stoves, the underwater goggles, and the medical kit comprising every malaria specific, dysentery remedy, antivenin, vitamin, ointment, lotion, plaster, poultice, and powder known to hypochondria. Our knottiest problem was what to do with the score of empty leatherette folders which had contained our travelers' checks. We finally presented them to our cabin steward in lieu of a tip and the poor fellow's emotion as he realized the extent of our generosity was pitiful. He just stood there and fumbled for words, many of which I am sure were familiar to us, but we thought it kinder to leave him to his own salvation and tiptoed out.

The arrival of the *Queen Mary* in New York, far from being the noisy, vivid pageant we expected, was as fleeting and elusive as an episode in a Kafka novel. Stealthily, almost as if fate begrudged us the satisfaction of seeing the harbor and the skyline, we were wafted from the open sea one evening to a North River pier the following dawn. The whole process was a grotesque mixture of the ephemeral and the banal; we descended the gangplank with no more illusion of having spanned the Atlantic than though we had commuted from Weehawken. It was only when our consorts and the fledglings streamed toward us from behind the barrier that our bewilderment abated. To say it disappeared entirely would be untrue; at one point in the resulting scrimmage, I discovered myself bussing a willowy showgirl under the impression that she was Hirschfeld's infant daughter, at another I was dandling a peppery old gentleman on my knee and quizzing him about his progress at school. At last, however, we managed to unsnarl our respective kinfolk, and after a breathless résumé of the fire, flood, and famine that had occurred in our absence, plunged into the ordeal of the customs examination.

Three quarters of an hour afterward, a fetching tableau might have presented itself to anyone sufficiently curious to invade the section bearing my initial. Knee-deep in a mound of shawls, brocades, bracelets, necklaces, purses, fans, and bric-a-brac resembling the contents of a thrift shop, three nonplused inspectors were attempting to calculate the duty I owed. My wife and I, our faces drawn, sat on the sidelines tonelessly discussing some practical solution to the dilemma—flight, a rubber check, a fifth mortgage on our home, selling the children. Under the circumstances, the last seemed the most feasible, inasmuch as they were loading the antique pistols I had bought them with percussion caps and discharging them into our eardrums. I am still not sure how I ever got off the hook, ex-

Full many a smuggler is born to blush unseen: the customs examination

cept that a few weeks afterward Hirschfeld showed me an I.O.U. with my name signed in a shaky scrawl. It was, needless to say, a blatant forgery and beneath contempt, but rather than see my friend victimized by some unscrupulous rascal, I shouldered the responsibility and settled with him for ten cents on the dollar.

Speeding across town from the pier to the family flat, I was dismayed to find hardly any civic recognition of our return; no bunting decked the buildings, almost no crowds clustered about the cab showering it with confetti and cheering hoarsely, and a minimum of brass bands lined the sidewalk before my residence. The sole member of the welcoming committee, a beery doorman chewing a half-dead cigar stump, eyed me with restrained enthusiasm as I sprang from the taxi. "Oh, *you're* back, are you?" he commented sourly. "Well, won't be long before I'll be carrying *you* upstairs four o'clock in the morning."

A similarly fervent salutation greeted me on entering our front door. The woolly little puppy I remembered cuddling in my arms, now grown to mastiff proportions, took one rapid sniff and zestfully sank his fangs into my ankle. By stroking him gently on the head with a length of chain, though, I won his confidence, and, dusting glass and shredded wallpaper from my shoulders, groped my way into the nest. Nothing was changed; the veneer on our installment furniture curled as crazily as ever and a disgruntled maid (not the one I recalled, but another equally morose) was stuffing herself with caviar and watering the whiskey. Subsequently I observed her comparing me furtively with my photograph on the piano and shaking her head. "Don't try and tell *me* that's the same man," I overheard her declaring to the broom. Whoever I was, she obviously thought me worthy of respect, because from then on she seldom ventured into my presence without a bread-knife concealed under her apron.

For the next week I filled a dubious role in the family unit, a cross between that of Santa Claus and a second-story worker. I was never certain, when I came through a doorway, whether my relatives would overwhelm me with caresses or recoil as from a phantom. Conditioned to the idea that I was mousing around in Asia or Africa, my proximity unnerved them. Even inanimate objects seemed to resent my presence; my clothes-closets were jammed with bicycles, vacuum-cleaners, mothproof bags, and corresponding household impedimenta that resisted any effort to dislodge them. The telephone rang constantly with what I supposed would be joyful greetings from friends but invariably proved to be the children's playmates and credit managers. Neither of the latter appeared to be enthralled by my adventures, and I finally decided that if they preferred to live in abysmal ignorance of the true state of the world, I personally had done my utmost by them.

No trip of the scope of ours, naturally, would have been complete without a motion-picture record, and Hirschfeld, an ardent cameraman, had exposed over four thousand feet of sixteen-millimeter film on the journey. On a brisk autumn evening in November, a select audience of two or three dozen friends crowded into my living room to witness the results. The party buzzed with anticipation; it was generally admitted that by all existing standards, this bade fair to be the outstanding travel picture of the decade. And in many respects it was. Though the greater part of it was upside down, backward, and out of focus, it had moments of breath-taking beauty—the traffic on Wilshire Boulevard in Los Angeles, the traffic on Hornby Road in Bombay, and the traffic in Leicester Square in London. In between were illimitable miles of shoreline in Siam and countless shots of monkeys picking fleas out of each other, interspersed here and there with gaudy sunsets. Unluckily for my commentary, I swallowed a poisoned highball halfway through it and confused many of the locales, a mischance that led to protracted bickering between the projectionist and myself. The audience tactfully muffled our squabble by yawning as loudly as it could, and everybody agreed that you would have to get up pretty early in the morning to find a more piquant film. Most of them were willing to try, nevertheless, and, since it was already way past nine o'clock, hurriedly took their leave. To show what degree of wanderlust the travelogue inspired, not a single one of those who saw it on that occasion was available for a second showing. They had all left town

within forty-eight hours, and I can only assume they must have set forth immediately for the romantic places we had visited.

One year from the day on which our project to circle the globe had been hatched, Hirschfeld and I sat in a chophouse off Broadway and solemnly clinked glasses. Our pilgrimage was over. Behind us lay the twenty-five thousand miles of desert, sea, and jungle we had traversed; we had trod a perilous course through wars, revolutions, uprisings, and insurrections; we had undergone greater extremes of heat and cold, seen more underprivileged people, and eaten worse food than either of us had dreamed existed. And now, looking at the whole thing in retrospect, we saw with incredulity that we had come through our adventure absolutely unscathed. In our faces was none of that rich harvest of serenity and wisdom, that fund of mellow philosophy to lighten the daily burden, and that broad tolerance for human frailty guaranteed to shine forth from the countenance of the returned traveler. If anything, we were more crabbed, pettifogging, and ornery than before we had set off.

"Yes, sir," murmured Hirschfeld, leaning back in the booth with a sigh, "it's been a glorious year—and do you know what I'd say if anyone offered me a million dollars to go through it again?" The words had hardly left his lips when a portly, well-to-do individual in a black Homburg, pince-nez, white piping on his vest, and gold-headed cane, strode up to the table.

"Have I the honor of addressing Mr. Hirschfeld?" he inquired.

"You have," returned Hirschfeld steadily.

"Capital," said the stranger, spreading his coat-tails. "Then we need not waste time in idle formalities. I have been delegated by a group of powerful men whose identity I may not reveal to ask you to go around the world. Realizing, of course, that you have other commitments, we are prepared to offer you this trifling emolument." He withdrew his wallet and extended a certified check for a million dollars. Hirschfeld arose, took the check, and carefully tore it into a dozen tiny pieces.

"That, sir, is my answer," he said, flinging them in the astounded emissary's face. He turned toward me, proffering his arm. "Shall we stroll?" he suggested. "The air has a rather pleasant tang this afternoon, don't you think?" And with a courtly bow to our would-be benefactor, we brushed past him into the eddying mass of humanity in Times Square.